Annette,

"Careful Playing
with Fire!".

PLAY WITH FIRE

IMAGES & INGREDIENTS THAT IGNITE

THE HUMAN PURSUIT OF PLEASURE-SOMETHING SO INNATE AND UNIVERSAL THAT IT IS PERHAPS SECOND ONLY TO THE QUEST FOR THE BASIC NEEDS TO EAT AND DRINK. WITH ITS ABILITY TO POWERFULLY ENGAGE THE SENSES, FOOD IS NOT ONLY ONE OF THESE ESSENTIALS TO SURVIVAL, BUT ALSO ONE OF LIFE'S MOST POWERFUL APHRODISIACS. IT SATIATES BOTH OUR HUNGER AND OUR PLEASURE CENTERS, PROVIDING INSTANT GRATIFICATION IN A NUMBER OF DIFFERENT WAYS.

PLAY WITH FIRE, DESIGNED ESPECIALLY FOR COUPLES OF ALL KINDS TO ENJOY TOGETHER, IS A DELICIOUS EXPLORATION OF THE UNMISTAKABLE CONNECTION BETWEEN FOOD AND SENSUALITY. IT AROUSES THE EYES WITH HIGH QUALITY SEDUCTIVE VISUALS FROM PROMINENT PHOTOGRAPHER ALAIN MARTINEZ AND THE PALATE WITH SIMPLE YET MOUTHWATERING MAXIMUM FLAVOR RECIPES FROM RENOWNED CULINARY ARTIST CHEF ADRIANNE CALVO. BY FACILITATING EQUAL PARTICIPATION IN THE PREPARATION OF TANTALIZING DISHES, **PLAY WITH FIRE** OFFERS THE EXPERIENCE OF THE INTOXICATING ANTICIPATION AND ENHANCED LEVEL OF INTIMACY THAT CAN ONLY COME FROM CO-CREATION OF SOMETHING AS STIMULATING AS FOOD.

ABOUT THE CHEF
ADRIANNE CALVO

CHEF ADRIANNE CALVO BEGAN BLAZING A TRAIL OF CULINARY INNOVATION AS A TEENAGER AND CONTINUALLY HAS REACHED NEW AND UNPRECEDENTED HEIGHTS EVER SINCE. DATING BACK TO HER YEARS AS ONE OF ACCLAIMED JOHNSON AND WALES UNIVERSITY'S MOST ACCOMPLISHED STUDENTS, CHEF ADRIANNE HAS CONSISTENTLY DISPLAYED A TALENT FOR TRULY "MAKING IT COUNT" DURING EACH AND EVERY ENDEAVOR IN THE KITCHEN. FROM SECURING MULTIPLE 1ST PLACE FINISHES IN THE RENOWNED INTERNATIONAL COMPETITION TASTE DOWN UNDER THAT RESULTED IN HER WINNING DISHES BEING SERVED TO THE UNITED NATIONS, CNN CORRESPONDENTS, AND FOOD NETWORK, BON APPETITE, AND GOURMET REPRESENTATIVES, TO CATERING THE LOCKER ROOM OF THE 2003 WORLD CHAMPION FLORIDA MARLINS AND BECOMING THE 5 DIAMOND MANDARIN ORIENTAL HOTEL 'S YOUNGEST CHEF EVER, CHEF ADRIANNE HAS UNDOUBTEDLY DEMONSTRATED A KNACK FOR NOT JUST MERELY MAKING A SPLASH, BUT A VIRTUAL TIDAL WAVE! AT THE BOLD AGE OF 23 AND READY TO BRING HER UNIQUE MAXIMUM FLAVOR STYLE TO THE MASSES, SHE OPENED HER HIGHLY REGARDED AND NAPA VALLEY-INSPIRED VINEYARD RESTAURANT AND WINE BAR CHEF ADRIANNES, WHERE SHE HAS CONSISTENTLY DELIGHTED HER PATRONS WITH TANTALIZING AND FLAVORFUL RECIPES WHILE PROVIDING THEM WITH EXOTIC NEW SETTINGS IN WHICH TO ENJOY THEM DURING HER IMMENSELY POPULAR DARK DINING EVENTS. 2014 SAW CHEF ADRIANNE ADD TO HER EXTENSIVE PORTFOLIO OF ACHIEVEMENTS BY CAPTURING THE PRESTIGIOUS BEST CHEF AWARD BY THE FLORIDIAN AWARDS III-CULINARY AWARDS, AS WELL AS HER PROMINENT ESTABLISHMENT BECOMING THE RECIPIENT OF A MIAMI MAGAZINE'S READER'S CHOICE AWARD FOR BEST RESTAURANT IN A CITY KNOWN FOR ITS VAST SELECTION OF QUALITY FINE DINING OPTIONS. EXPANDING THE SEEMINGLY LIMITLESS REACH OF HER TALENTS TO THE WORLD OF MULTI-MEDIA, CHEF ADRIANNE ALSO RECENTLY DEBUTED HER GROUNDBREAKING FOOD AS A LIFESTYLE ONLINE TV SERIES AND HAS CO-HOSTED THE VASTLY POPULAR MAXIMUM FLAVOR LIVE SEGMENT ON NBC MIAMI SINCE 2011, ALONG WITH BEING FEATURED ON A VARIETY OF REGIONAL AND NATIONAL TALK SHOWS. ON THE HEELS OF THE DECEMBER 2014 RELEASE OF HER UNIQUE, OUTSIDE-THE-BOX COOKBOOK #MAXIMUMFLAVORSOCIAL, CHEF ADRIANNE NOW TURNS HER FIERY PASSION AND DRIVE INTO MAKING HER PALATE PLEASURING MAXIMUM FLAVOR RECIPES AN INTEGRAL PART OF ANOTHER BREAKTHROUGH CREATIVE VENTURE, **PLAY WITH FIRE**.

ABOUT THE ARTIST
ALAIN MARTINEZ

ALAIN MARTINEZ IS AN INTERNATIONAL BEAUTY AND WEDDING PHOTOGRAPHER, INSTRUCTOR AND AUTHOR. BORN IN 1980, ALAIN DID NOT PICK UP HIS FIRST CAMERA UNTIL 2005 IN PARIS AND HAS NEVER PUT IT DOWN AFTER THAT. SINCE THEN HIS UNIQUE STYLE AND KEEN ATTENTION TO DETAIL HAS COMMISSIONED HIM BY THE MOST DISCERNING CLIENTS TO CAPTURE THEIR MOST CHERISHED MOMENTS AROUND THE WORLD – LITERALLY. ALAIN FEELS FORTUNATE TO HAVE TRAVELED ALL OVER FRANCE, ITALY, GREECE, SPAIN, UKRAINE, SWITZERLAND, SOUTH AND CENTRAL AMERICA AND OTHER PLACES AS FAR AS NORWAY TO PHOTOGRAPH CLIENTS THAT UNDERSTAND THE VALUE OF HIS UNIQUENESS AND MENTOR PHOTOGRAPHERS THAT WANT TO ELEVATE THEIR CRAFT. HIS WORK IS PERCEIVED BY MANY AS SYNONYMOUS OF SEXY AND CLASSY AND CLIENTS VISIT HIS STUDIO FROM ALL OVER THE NATION FOR AN OPPORTUNITY TO FEEL AND LOOK LIKE A BOMBSHELL.

ALAIN'S WORK HAS BEEN FEATURED ALL OVER THE UNITED STATES IN MAGAZINES SUCH AS WEDDING STYLE, RANGE FINDER MAGAZINE, OCEAN DRIVE, SELECTA AND MULTIPLE OTHER PUBLICATIONS AND MEDIA OUTLETS SUCH AS DECO DRIVE AND VARIOUS NEWS CHANNELS.

AS A MAN WHO CONSIDERS HIMSELF GIFTED IN NON-MATERIAL THINGS, HE UNDERSTANDS THAT THERE ARE MANY PEOPLE LESS FORTUNATE WHO NEED HELP, WHICH MAKES PHILANTHROPY A FOREMOST EFFORT FOR ALAIN MARTINEZ AND HIS STAFF. HE HAS BEEN INVOLVED WITH HIS HOUSE, MIAMI CHILDREN'S FOUNDATION, ST. JUDE AND MANY OTHER REPUTABLE NON-PROFIT FOUNDATIONS TO BRIGHTEN UP THE LIVES OF CHILDREN IN HIS COMMUNITY.

ABOVE ALL HIS NUMBER ONE PRIORITY IN LIFE IS HIS FAMILY. ALAIN SPENDS HIS FREE TIME WITH HIS WIFE AND TWO CHILDREN IN MIAMI AND AROUND THE WORLD--THE STARS OF THE POPULAR HASHTAG #JUSTTWOBROSIN, TWO BROTHERS TRAVELING THE WORLD. HIS FAMILY KEEPS HIM GROUNDED AND INSPIRED TO BE ENDLESSLY PASSIONATE ABOUT HIS CRAFT AND THE BELIEF OF HELPING THOSE IN NEED. HIS RESPECT, WORLD CLASS ETHICS AND GENEROSITY TOWARD HIS CLIENTS ARE ONLY SURPASSED BY HIS PROMISE TO CAPTURE UNREPEATABLE MOMENTS IN THE MOST ARTISTIC WAY AND TURN THEM INTO TIMELESS PIECES OF FAMILY HEIRLOOMS FOR GENERATIONS TO COME.

LIBATION

22 COCONUT WATER-MELON **ELIXIR**

40 **WAVES** OF **WATERMELON**

73 **FORBIDDEN** LOVE

DATE **NIGHT**

25 **MARINATED** ARTICHOKE HEARTS

29 **FANCY** FIGS

37 STRAWBERRY AVOCADO AND **PECAN SALAD**

38 SPICY WATERMELON AND **SERRANO HAM**

42 **LINGUINE** WITH ALMOND **PESTO**

45 **HOT** AND **SWEET** NUTS

49 **GREEK** OLIVE **PUFF**

DATE **NIGHT**
CONTINUED...

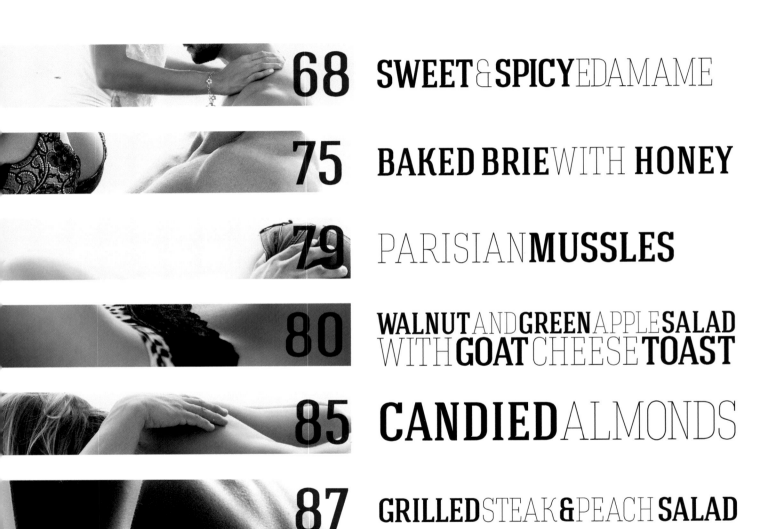

THEREAFTER...

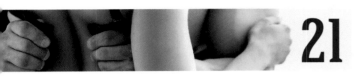

LET'S MAKE BREAKFAST

33 ASPARAGUS FRITTATA

66 LOBSTER EGGS BENEDICT

76 SMOKED SALMON CREAM **CHEESE** AND **CHIVE** OMELETTE

HOTCANDIED **BACON** 83

BLUEBERRYBUTTERMILK PANCAKES**WITH** BOURBON MAPLE SYRUP 103

CORNAND**QUESO** BREAKFAST **BURRITO** 107

SWEET ONION, HAM&CHEESE FRITTATA 117

RASPBERRY AND
PISTACHIO SEMIFREDDO

SERVES 2

SPECIAL EQUIPMENT: LOAF PAN, PLASTIC WRAP

INGREDIENTS

6 EGG YOLKS

3 TABLESPOONS HONEY

1 CUP HEAVY CREAM, WHIPPED

2 TEASPOONS ROSEWATER

1 TEASPOON PURE VANILLA EXTRACT

1/2 PINT FRESH RASPBERRIES, PLUS EXTRA FOR GARNISH

3 TABLESPOONS SHELLED PISTACHIO NUTS, CHOPPED

DIRECTIONS

LOVER A. LINE THE BASE AND TWO SIDES OF THE LOAF PAN WITH A SHEET OF PLASTIC WRAP, LEAVING A GENEROUS AMOUNT OF THE WRAP HANGING OVER THE SIDES OF THE PAN.

LOVER B. DRIZZLE THE HONEY INTO THE BROKEN EGG YOLKS AND THEN WHIP THE MIXTURE WITH AN ELECTRIC BEATER FOR 10 MINUTES OR UNTIL IT IS PALE YELLOW IN COLOR. IT SHOULD BE THICK, SMOOTH AND CREAMY.

LOVER A. GENTLY FOLD IN THE WHIPPED CREAM, ROSEWATER, AND VANILLA. ADD THE RASPBERRIES, PISTACHIOS, AND FOLD THE PLASTIC OVER THE TOP TO COVER THE SEMIFREDDO.

FREEZE UNTIL DESSERT IS COMPLETELY FROZEN ABOUT 4 HOURS. BEFORE SERVING, TRANSFER TO THE REFRIGERATOR TO SOFTEN, ABOUT 20 MINUTES. TURN THE DESSERT OUT OF THE PAN, AND SLICE IT AND GARNISH WITH EXTRA RASPBERRIES.

COCONUT WATER-
MELON ELIXIR

SERVES 2

INGREDIENTS

2 CUPS ICE

THE COCONUT WATER FROM 1 WHOLE CHILLED FRESH COCONUT

1 WHOLE CHILLED FRESH LIME, JUICE ONLY

1 WHOLE ASIAN PEAR, CHILLED AND SLICED

1/2 CHILLED CUCUMBER

1/4 CUP CHILLED ALOE JUICE

SUGAR, TO TASTE

DIRECTIONS

LOVER A. KEEP ALL INGREDIENTS (EXCEPT THE SUGAR) ICY-COLD IN THE REFRIGERATOR OVERNIGHT, UNTIL YOU ARE READY TO PREPARE THIS REFRESHING THIRST-QUENCHER. GLASSES SHOULD BE ICED IN THE FREEZER.

LOVER B. POUR ALL INGREDIENTS INTO A BLENDER AND WHIP UP A SLUSHIE.

LOVER A. ADD SUGAR TO TASTE IF NEEDED. POUR INTO TWO ICED GLASSES. ENJOY.

MARINATED
ARTICHOKE HEARTS

SERVES 2

INGREDIENTS

1 9-OUNCE BOX FROZEN ARTICHOKE HEARTS, THAWED

1/2 CUP EXTRA-VIRGIN OLIVE OIL

KOSHER SALT

1/2 TEASPOON DRIED THYME

1/2 TEASPOON DRIED OREGANO

1/4 TEASPOON CRUSHED RED PEPPER FLAKES

2 TABLESPOONS FRESHLY-SQUEEZED LEMON JUICE

DIRECTIONS

LOVER A. RINSE ARTICHOKE HEARTS UNDER COLD WATER, AND PAT DRY. BRING THE OIL TO A SIZZLE IN A SAUCEPAN SET OVER MEDIUM HEAT.

LOVER B. ADD THE ARTICHOKES, SALT, THYME, OREGANO, AND PEPPER FLAKES. COVER AND COOK, STIRRING OCCASIONALLY, UNTIL THE FLAVORS HAVE INTERMINGLED, ABOUT 10 MINUTES.

LET COOL TO ROOM TEMPERATURE AND STIR IN LEMON JUICE. REFRIGERATE FOR 4 TO 6 HOURS. STIR AGAIN AND SERVE AT ROOM TEMPERATURE.

BANANAS FOSTERS

SERVES 2

SPECIAL EQUIPMENT: LONG MATCHES, LIKE THE ONES YOU USE TO LIGHT THE FIREPLACE.

INGREDIENTS

1/4 CUP UNSALTED BUTTER

1 CUP PACKED BROWN SUGAR

1/4 CUP CRÈME DE BANANE (BANANA LIQUEUR)

1/2 TEASPOON GROUND CINNAMON

2 FIRM, RIPE BANANAS

1/4 CUP DARK RUM

PINCH OF FLEUR DE SEL, OR SEA SALT

2 CUPS VANILLA ICE CREAM

DIRECTIONS

LOVER A. MELT THE BUTTER IN A LARGE NONSTICK SKILLET OVER MEDIUM HEAT. STIR IN BROWN SUGAR, LIQUEUR, AND CINNAMON. BRING TO A SIMMER AND COOK FOR 3 MINUTES, STIRRING OCCASIONALLY.

LOVER B. WHILE YOUR PARTNER IS COOKING THE MIXTURE, PEEL THE BANANAS AND CUT EACH IN HALF LENGTHWISE. CUT EACH HALF INTO 2 PIECES. FIND THE BOTTLE OF COGNAC AND THE RUM.

LOVER A. SLIDE THE BANANAS INTO THE PAN AND SIMMER FOR 4 TO 5 MINUTES OR UNTIL THE BANANAS ARE TENDER TO THE TOUCH. REMOVE FROM THE HEAT. DIG UP A PAIR OF COGNAC SNIFTERS.

LOVER B. ADD THE RUM TO THE PAN, AND IGNITE WITH A LONG MATCH. STIR BANANAS GENTLY UNTIL THE FLAME DIES DOWN. THERE SHOULD BE PLENTY OF HEAT, SO TAKE CARE. STOKE THE FLAME IN THE FIREPLACE WHILE…

LOVER A. …SPOONS THE BANANA MIXTURE OVER THE ICE CREAM AND SPRINKLES ALL WITH A TOUCH OF FLEUR DE SEL. THIS SENSUAL SWEET CAN BE SERVED IN TWO DISHES…OR BETTER YET, ENJOY IT IN ONE DISH WITH TWO SPOONS AND TWO SNIFTERS OF COGNAC, LOUNGING ON THROW CUSHIONS BEFORE THE CRACKLING FIRE.

FANCY
FIGS

SERVES 2

FOR FANCY PEOPLE WHO KNOW HOW TO LIVE AND LOVE AND EAT

INGREDIENTS

12 DRIED FIGS

1-1/2 OUNCES SOFTENED CREAM CHEESE (HALF A 3-OUNCE PACKAGE)

1 TABLESPOON POWDERED SUGAR

2 TEASPOONS ORANGE LIQUEUR

12 ROASTED, SALTED ALMONDS

DIRECTIONS

LOVER A. CUT A SLIT IN THE LARGE SIDE OF EACH FIG, CUTTING ALMOST BUT NOT THROUGH TO THE STEM.

LOVER B. BLEND TOGETHER THE CREAM CHEESE, POWDERED SUGAR, AND ORANGE LIQUEUR UNTIL GOOEY AND CREAMY.

LOVERS A AND B. USING A SPOON AND YOUR FINGERS FILL EACH FIG EVENLY WITH THE CREAM CHEESE MIXTURE AND 1 ALMOND. PRESS FIGS WITH YOUR FINGERS TO MAKE SURE FILLING IS IN TIGHTLY.

LOVENOTE: PROCEED TO LICK FINGERS IN ANY COMBINATION OF AA, BB, BA OR AB, AND ENJOY YOUR FANCY FIGS.

WHITE CHOCOLATE DIPPED
RED ROSE PETALS

SERVES 10

THIS SEXY TREAT MUST BE ACCOMPANIED BY A GLOW OF CANDLELIGHT AND A BOTTLE OF BEAUJOLAIS.

INGREDIENTS
2-3 RED ROSES, UNSPRAYED
4 OUNCES HIGH QUALITY WHITE CHOCOLATE, CHOPPED OR IN PIECES
HAWAIIAN PINK SALT, FOR SPRINKLING

DIRECTIONS
LOVER A. CAREFULLY TRIM THE ROSE PETALS FROM THE FLOWER BULB IN ORDER TO HAVE INDIVIDUAL PETALS.

LOVER B. SET UP A DOUBLE BOILER BY PLACING A HEAT-PROOF BOWL OVER A MEDIUM SAUCE POT WITH AN INCH OR TWO OF BOILING WATER. KEEP THE WATER SIMMERING (BUT NOT BOILING) WHILE YOU SPILL THE WHITE CHOCOLATE PIECES INTO THE BOWL. AS THE CHOCOLATE MELTS USE A RUBBER SPATULA TO STIR CONSTANTLY, SCRAPING DOWN THE EDGES OF THE BOWL, BEING CAREFUL NOT TO LET THE CHOCOLATE BURN.

LOVER A. ONCE THE CHOCOLATE IS SMOOTH AND VELVETY, REMOVE THE BOWL FROM DOUBLE BOILER. DIP EACH INDIVIDUAL PETAL INTO THE SMOOTH WHITE CHOCOLATE AND SET ON A NONSTICK COOKIE SHEET TO HARDEN.

LOVER B. BEFORE THE WHITE CHOCOLATE HARDENS, SPRINKLE LIGHTLY WITH HAWAIIAN PINK SALT.

LOVENOTE: THESE WILL KEEP, REFRIGERATED, FOR UP TO TWO DAYS...BUT WHY WAIT? HAVE ANOTHER BITE WITH A SIP OF THE BEAUJOLAIS.

ASPARAGUS
FRITTATA

SERVES 4

INGREDIENTS

12 LARGE EGGS, BEATEN
1/2 CUP HEAVY CREAM
1/2 CUP PARMESAN CHEESE, GRATED
2 TABLESPOONS BUTTER
2 TABLESPOONS EXTRA-VIRGIN OLIVE OIL
1 ONION, DICED
1/2 POUND THIN PENCIL ASPARAGUS, BLANCHED IN BOILING WATER, CHILLED AND DICED
1 TABLESPOON CHIVES, MINCED
1 TABLESPOON THYME, MINCED
KOSHER SALT AND FRESHLY GROUND BLACK PEPPER

DIRECTIONS

LOVER A. HEAT THE OVEN TO 350. IN A LARGE BOWL COMBINE THE BEATEN EGGS WITH THE CREAM AND PARMESAN. HEAT THE BUTTER WITH THE OIL IN A LARGE SAUTÉ PAN OVER MEDIUM HIGH HEAT.

LOVER B. ADD THE ONION, LOWER THE HEAT AND COOK, STIRRING OCCASIONALLY, UNTIL THE ONION IS SIZZLING GOLDEN, ABOUT 4 OR 5 MINUTES.

LOVER A. USING A LARGE WOODEN SPATULA, STIR THE EGGS INTO THE SKILLET AND TURN THE HEAT DOWN LOW. STIR THE EGG MIXTURE TO FORM A LARGE FLAT OMELET SHAPE, FULLY COVERING THE BOTTOM OF THE PAN. WHEN THE EGGS BEGIN TO COOK AND TAKE SHAPE, STIR IN THE DICED ASPARAGUS AND THE HERBS. GET THE CHAMPAGNE FROM THE FRIDGE AND SQUEEZE A COUPLE OF FRESH ORANGES.

LOVER B. PLACE THE SAUTÉ PAN IN THE HOT OVEN AND CONTINUE TO COOK FOR 2 TO 3 MORE MINUTES, OR UNTIL THE FRITTATA IS COOKED AROUND THE EDGES AND THE CENTER HAS PUFFED UP. REMOVE FROM THE OVEN AND INVERT ONTO A LARGE PLATE.

LOVERS A AND B. PREPARE MIMOSAS WITH THE FRESHLY-SQUEEZED ORANGE JUICE AND A SPLASH OR TWO OF CHAMPAGNE. ARRANGE THEM ON A NAPKIN-COVERED TRAY WITH THE FRITTATA, CLOTH NAPKINS AND A BUD VASE WITH ROSEBUDS, AND CARRY YOUR PICNIC TO BED.

LOVENOTE WARNING: ASPARAGUS NATURALLY INCREASES HORMONE PRODUCTION…

DECADENT
CHOCOLATE MOUSSE

SERVES 2

GET OUT THE CHILLED CHAMPAGNE.

INGREDIENTS

9 OUNCES SEMISWEET CHOCOLATE, FINELY CHOPPED

4 1/2 TABLESPOONS UNSALTED BUTTER, CUT INTO SMALL CUBES

2 TABLESPOONS STRONG-BREWED ESPRESSO

6 LARGE EGGS, SEPARATED

3 TABLESPOONS SUGAR

2 CUPS HEAVY CREAM, CHILLED

1/4 TEASPOON PURE VANILLA EXTRACT

CHOCOLATE SHAVINGS, FOR GARNISH

DIRECTIONS

LOVER A. GET A FEW INCHES OF WATER SIMMERING IN THE BOTTOM OF A DOUBLE BOILER. IN THE TOP HALF OR A BOWL PLACED DIRECTLY ON THE POT OF WATER, COMBINE THE CHOCOLATE, BUTTER AND ESPRESSO. COOK OVER MODERATELY LOW HEAT, STIRRING, UNTIL THE CHOCOLATE IS MELTED. UNCORK THE CHAMPAGNE.

LOVER B. REMOVE THE TOP OF THE DOUBLE BOILER AND SET IT AWAY FROM THE HEAT TO LET THE CHOCOLATE COOL FOR ABOUT 10 TO 15 MINUTES. YOU MIGHT STICK THE TIP OF YOUR FINGER INTO THE COOLED CHOCOLATE FOR A TASTE. FOLLOW UP WITH A SIP OF CHAMPAGNE. SHARE THIS WITH YOUR LOVER.

LOVER A. BEAT THE EGG YOLKS INTO THE CHOCOLATE AND STIR UNTIL INCORPORATED.

LOVER B. IN A LARGE BOWL, BEAT THE EGG WHITES AT MEDIUM-HIGH SPEED UNTIL SOFT PEAKS FORM. SLOWLY ADD THE SUGAR AND BEAT UNTIL THE WHITES ARE SLIGHTLY FIRM AND GLOSSY. TAKE CARE NOT TO OVER-BEAT OR THE WHITES WILL BE DRY.

LOVER A. IN ANOTHER BOWL, BEAT THE CREAM WITH THE VANILLA EXTRACT UNTIL FIRM.

LOVERS A AND B. GENTLY FOLD HALF OF THE WHIPPED CREAM INTO THE CHOCOLATE MIXTURE, THEN FOLD IN HALF OF THE BEATEN WHITES UNTIL NO STREAKS REMAIN. REPEAT WITH THE REMAINING WHITES AND WHIPPED CREAM.

LOVENOTE: FOR A TOUCH OF ELEGANCE, SPOON THE MOUSSE INTO STEM GLASSES AND REFRIGERATE FOR AT LEAST 3 HOURS. GARNISH WITH CHOCOLATE SHAVINGS AND SERVE CHILLED. WITH THE REMAINING CHAMPAGNE, IF THERE'S ANY LEFT. BETTER YET, WITH A GOOD QUALITY ZINFANDEL OR CABERNET SAUVIGNON. A WINE THAT BOLD CAN HOLD UP TO THE FLAVOR OF CHOCOLATE AND HIGHLIGHT ITS NOTES.

STRAWBERRY AVOCADO AND PECAN SALAD

SERVES 2

POUR YOURSELVES A GLASS OF SAUTERNES WINE. THIS DELICIOUS FRENCH WINE IS CHARACTERIZED BY ITS SPICY BLEND OF SWEETNESS AND ACIDITY. COUPLED WITH THIS NUTTY SALAD, IT'S A MATCH MADE IN HEAVEN!

INGREDIENTS

2 TABLESPOONS WHITE SUGAR
2 TABLESPOONS OLIVE OIL
4 TEASPOONS HONEY
1 TABLESPOON BALSAMIC OR RASPBERRY VINEGAR
1 TEASPOON FRESH LEMON JUICE
KOSHER SALT AND FRESHLY GROUND PEPPER, TO TASTE
2 CUPS ORGANIC MIXED GREENS
1 RIPE AVOCADO, PEELED, PITTED AND DICED
10 FRESH, RIPE STRAWBERRIES, SLICED
1/2 CUP CHOPPED PECANS, LIGHTLY TOASTED

DIRECTIONS

LOVER A. TO PREPARE THE DRESSING WHISK TOGETHER THE SUGAR, HONEY, VINEGAR, AND LEMON JUICE IN A SMALL BOWL. SLOWLY TRICKLE IN THE OLIVE OIL AND CONTINUE WHISKING BETWEEN TRICKLES. SEASON WITH SALT AND PEPPER AND SET ASIDE.

LOVER B. PLACE THE GREENS IN A SERVING BOWL AND TOP WITH AVOCADO AND STRAWBERRIES. DRIZZLE THE DRESSING OVER EVERYTHING, THEN SPRINKLE WITH PECANS.

LOVENOTE: THIS SALAD, LIKE THE WINE, AND LIKE MOST RELATIONSHIPS, IS A DELICATE BALANCE OF SWEETNESS AND THE DELICIOUS SURPRISE OF A TANGY BITE.

SPICY WATERMELON AND SERRANO HAM

SERVES 2

AN UNUSUAL AMALGAM OF FLAVORS TO THRILL YOUR TASTEBUDS.

INGREDIENTS

1 TEASPOON CRUSHED RED PEPPER FLAKES

1 TEASPOON CORIANDER SEEDS

1 CUP WHITE WINE VINEGAR

1 CUP WATER

1/2 CUP SUGAR

3 PIECES LEMON RIND

1/4 SEEDLESS WATERMELON, PEELED AND CUBED

1/2 CANTALOUPE, PEELED AND CUBED

8 THIN SLICES SERRANO HAM

1 CUP MIXED GOOD OLIVES, PREFERABLY MANZANILLAS, KALAMATAS

EXTRA VIRGIN OLIVE OIL, FOR DRIZZLING

KOSHER SALT

DIRECTIONS

LOVER A. PREPARE THE PICKLING LIQUID: IN A MEDIUM SAUCEPAN COMBINE THE CRUSHED RED PEPPER FLAKES, CORIANDER SEEDS, VINEGAR, WATER, SUGAR AND LEMON RIND. SET THE PAN OVER MEDIUM HEAT, AND SIMMER FOR 3 MINUTES.

LOVER B. DROP THE WATERMELON AND CANTALOUPE CUBES INTO THE PICKLING LIQUID. ALLOW THE MELON TO PICKLE FOR ABOUT 3 MINUTES TO ALLOW THE EXOTIC FLAVORS TO INFUSE THE FLESH LIGHTLY.

LOVERS A. AND B. TO SERVE, LAY THE SLICES OF HAM IN THE CENTER OF A SERVING PLATE AND TOP WITH A MOUND OF THE PICKLED MELONS. SCATTER THE OLIVES AROUND THE MELONS, DRIZZLE WITH THE OLIVE OIL AND ADD KOSHER SALT TO TASTE.

LOVENOTE: WITH ITS SURPRISING FLAVORS, THIS NOSH WILL THROW A PARTY IN YOUR MOUTH!

WAVES OF WATERMELON

SERVES 2

SPECIAL EQUIPMENT: COCKTAIL SHAKER AND STRAINER, CHILLED MARTINI GLASSES

INGREDIENTS

6 OUNCES CITRON VODKA

2 OUNCES WATERMELON LIQUEUR

1 OUNCE TRIPLE SEC

1 OUNCE LEMONADE

1 OUNCE LEMON LIME SODA

FRESH WATERMELON SLICE

DIRECTIONS

LOVER A. MIX ALL INGREDIENTS TOGETHER OVER ICE, SHAKE, AND STRAIN INTO CHILLED MARTINI GLASSES.

LOVER B. GARNISH EACH WITH A SLICE OF WATERMELON.

LOVENOTE: PACK A COOLER WITH ALL THE INGREDIENTS AND EQUIPMENT, AND ENJOY THESE AT THE BEACH IN YOUR OWN MIDSUMMER NIGHT'S DREAM. JUST THE TWO OF YOU.

LINGUINE WITH ALMOND PESTO

SERVES 2

ALTHOUGH PESTO IS OFTEN MADE WITH PINE NUTS, OR PIGNOLI, THE ALMONDS GIVE THIS DISH A NEW DIMENSION.

INGREDIENTS

KOSHER SALT
3/4 POUND ASPARAGUS, TRIMMED
2 CUPS GRAPE TOMATOES
1/2 CUP EXTRA-VIRGIN OLIVE OIL, IN ALL
1/2 CUP SLICED ALMONDS
1/4 CUP FRESH BASIL LEAVES
1 TABLESPOON GARLIC, MINCED
1/2 CUP PARMESAN CHEESE
1 LB. DRY LINGUINE
FRESHLY GROUND BLACK PEPPER

DIRECTIONS

LOVER A. PREHEAT THE OVEN TO 425 DEGREES. BRING A LARGE POT OF SALTED WATER TO A BOIL OVER HIGH HEAT.

LOVER B. ARRANGE THE ASPARAGUS IN A SINGLE LAYER ON ONE HALF OF A LARGE RIMMED BAKING SHEET. ARRANGE THE TOMATOES ON THE OTHER HALF OF THE SHEET. DRIZZLE BOTH WITH ¼ CUP OF THE OLIVE OIL, SEASON WITH 1/4 TEASPOON OF THE SALT, AND TOSS TO COAT. ROAST UNTIL THE TOMATOES HAVE BLISTERED AND THE ASPARAGUS ARE BRIGHT GREEN, ABOUT 20-25 MINUTES. REMOVE FROM THE HEAT AND SET ASIDE.

LOVER A. PLACE THE ALMONDS IN A FOOD PROCESSOR. ROUGHLY CHOP THE ASPARAGUS AND ADD TO THE FOOD PROCESSOR ALONG WITH THE BASIL, GARLIC, CHEESE, 1/2 TEASPOON OF THE SALT, AND THE REMAINING ¼ CUP OLIVE OIL. PULSE UNTIL A COARSE PASTE FORMS, ABOUT 10 SECONDS. SEASON TO TASTE WITH SALT AND PEPPER AND TRANSFER TO A LARGE SERVING BOWL.

LOVER B. COOK THE LINGUINE IN THE BOILING WATER ACCORDING TO PACKAGE DIRECTIONS UNTIL AL DENTE. WHILE THE PASTA IS COOKING, GRAB SOME WINE GLASSES AND A BOTTLE OF CRISP PINOT GRIGIO.

LOVER A. DRAIN THE PASTA, RESERVING 1/2 CUP OF THE PASTA COOKING WATER. STIR THE WATER INTO THE PESTO, ADD THE PASTA AND TOSS TO COAT.

LOVENOTE: THIS WILL BE FUN IF YOU BOTH EAT FROM THE BIG BOWL, SIPPING PINOT GRIGIO AND WATCHING AN OLD MARCELLO MASTROIANNI MOVIE.

HOT AND SWEET NUTS

SERVES 2

INGREDIENTS

3 TABLESPOONS HONEY
1 1/2 TABLESPOONS SUGAR
1 TABLESPOON MELTED BUTTER
1/2 TEASPOON SALT
1/2 TEASPOON CAYENNE PEPPER
2 CUPS SHELLED, UNSALTED NUTS

DIRECTIONS

LOVER A. HEAT THE OVEN TO 300 DEGREES. IN A BOWL MIX THE HONEY, SUGAR, BUTTER, SALT AND CAYENNE. ADD THE NUTS AND MIX WELL TO COAT.

LOVER B. TURN THE NUT MIXTURE INTO A BUTTERED 9- BY 13-INCH PAN AND PAT DOWN WITH A RUBBER SPATULA TO MAKE LEVEL. BAKE, SHAKING THE PAN OFTEN, UNTIL NUTS ARE GOLDEN BROWN, ABOUT 20 TO 25 MINUTES.

LOVER A. SCRAPE THE NUTS ONTO A BUTTERED 10- BY 12-INCH PIECE OF FOIL. ALLOW THE MIXTURE TO COOL FOR ABOUT 15 MINUTES.

LOVER B. BREAK THE BRITTLE INTO MEDIUM-SIZE PIECES.

LOVENOTE: CRUNCH, IF YOU DARE. YOU'LL HAVE A MOUTHFUL OF HEAT AND SWEET ALL AT ONCE.

COCOA ESPRESSO
TRUFFLES

SERVES 2

OH YES!

INGREDIENTS

1 CUP HEAVY CREAM
1 TABLESPOON INSTANT ESPRESSO POWDER
8 OUNCES SEMISWEET CHOCOLATE, CHOPPED
UNSWEETENED COCOA POWDER FOR DUSTING

DIRECTIONS

LOVER A. IN A MEDIUM SAUCEPAN OVER MEDIUM HEAT, HEAT THE CREAM UNTIL IT JUST STARTS TO STEAM AND BUBBLE SLIGHTLY ALONG THE EDGES. REMOVE IMMEDIATELY FROM THE HEAT.

LOVER B. QUICKLY STIR IN THE INSTANT ESPRESSO UNTIL IT DISSOLVES. POUR THE HOT CREAM AND ESPRESSO MIXTURE OVER THE CHOPPED CHOCOLATE IN A BOWL, AND STIR UNTIL THE CHOCOLATE IS COMPLETELY MELTED AND INCORPORATED INTO THE CREAM. ALLOW THIS GANACHE TO COOL TO ROOM TEMPERATURE AND THEN PLACE IN THE REFRIGERATOR TO CHILL FOR AT LEAST TWO HOURS UNTIL IT IS COMPLETELY FIRM. WHILE IT IS CHILLING, UNCORK A BOTTLE OF GOOD RED WINE, SUCH AS A CABERNET SAUVIGNON.

LOVER A. LINE A BAKING SHEET WITH WAXED PAPER AND SPRINKLE WITH THE COCOA POWDER. REMOVE THE CHOCOLATE MIXTURE FROM THE FRIDGE, AND USING A MELON BALLER SCOOP OUT BALLS OF GANACHE.

LOVER B. USE YOUR HANDS TO QUICKLY SHAPE THEM INTO SMOOTH BALLS. SERVE IMMEDIATELY OR STORE THEM IN AN AIRTIGHT CONTAINER IN THE FRIDGE FOR UP TO ONE WEEK.

LOVENOTE: YOU LOVERCOOKS DESERVE A REWARD FOR YOUR EFFORT, SO DON'T STORE THE TRUFFLES UNTIL YOU'VE SAMPLED AS MANY AS YOU LIKE. AND DON'T FORGET TO LICK YOUR FINGERS.

GREEK OLIVE
PUFF

SERVES 2

PUFFY AND SPICY AND JUST A LITTLE BIT SEXY, NIBBLE THESE OFF TOOTHPICKS, OR USE YOUR FINGERS; THEY ARE GUARANTEED TO GET YOUR APPETITE GOING!

INGREDIENTS

12 PITTED GREEK OLIVES
1 PACKAGE FROZEN PUFF PASTRY, THAWED

DIRECTIONS

LOVER A. HEAT OVEN TO 400 DEGREES F. CUT THE PASTRY INTO STRIPS ABOUT 6 INCHES LONG AND 1/2 INCH WIDE.

LOVER B. WRAP A BELT OF PASTRY AROUND EACH OLIVE. PLACE ON AN UNGREASED BAKING SHEET AND BAKE FOR 20 MINUTES, OR UNTIL THE PASTRY IS PUFFED AND GOLDEN BROWN.

LOVENOTE: NEVER HAVE TWO INGREDIENTS MEAN SO MUCH TO TWO LOVERS.

GINGER
ASPARAGUS
SERVES 2

INGREDIENTS

2 TEASPOONS CANOLA OIL
1/2 POUND FRESH ASPARAGUS, TRIMMED
2 TEASPOONS MINCED FRESH GINGER
1 TEASPOON MINCED FRESH GARLIC
1/2 TEASPOON SUGAR
1/4 TEASPOON KOSHER SALT
1/4 TEASPOON FRESHLY GROUND BLACK PEPPER
1 TEASPOON SESAME OIL

DIRECTIONS

LOVER A. HEAT THE OIL IN A LARGE NONSTICK SKILLET, AND SAUTÉ THE ASPARAGUS OVER MEDIUM-HIGH HEAT, 7 TO 8 MINUTES, TURNING THE STALKS OCCASIONALLY TO BROWN THEM EVENLY.

LOVER B. LOWER THE HEAT TO MEDIUM AND ADD THE GINGER AND GARLIC. SAUTÉ 1 TO 2 MINUTES, STIRRING OCCASIONALLY, TAKING CARE NOT TO LET THE GARLIC BURN.

LOVER A. STIR IN SUGAR, SALT, PEPPER AND SESAME OIL AND COOK FOR 1 MORE MINUTE, WHILE YOUR LOVER LIGHTS THE CANDLES ON THE TABLE...

LOVENOTE: COOL THE ASPARAGUS SLIGHTLY AND EAT EACH STALK WITH YOUR FINGERS IN THE FLICKERING CANDLELIGHT.

HONEY POMEGRANATE GLAZED CHICKEN THIGHS

SERVES 2

THIS IS OFFICIALLY CLASSIFIED AS LICK-YOUR-FINGERS FOOD.

INGREDIENTS

3/4 CUP HONEY
1/3 CUP FINELY CHOPPED SHALLOTS
1/4 CUP FRESH LEMON JUICE
1 TABLESPOON GRATED LEMON RIND
2 TABLESPOONS POMEGRANATE MOLASSES
1 TEASPOON WORCESTERSHIRE SAUCE
1 TEASPOON HOT SAUCE
4 GARLIC CLOVES, MINCED
4 CHICKEN THIGHS, SKINNED
1 TABLESPOON CORNSTARCH
1 TABLESPOON WATER
COOKING SPRAY
1 TEASPOON KOSHER SALT
1/4 TEASPOON FRESHLY GROUND BLACK PEPPER

DIRECTIONS

LOVER A. COMBINE THE FIRST 9 INGREDIENTS IN A LARGE BOWL. ADD THE CHICKEN THIGHS, COVERING THEM THOROUGHLY WITH THE MIXTURE. COVER AND MARINATE IN REFRIGERATOR FOR 2 TO 3 HOURS, WHILE YOU AND YOUR LOVER ENJOY SOME GOOD WINE AND MELLOW JAZZ.

LOVER B. HEAT UP THE OVEN TO 425∞. REMOVE THE CHICKEN FROM THE BOWL, RESERVING MARINADE. COMBINE CORNSTARCH AND WATER IN A SMALL BOWL.

LOVER A. POUR THE RESERVED MARINADE INTO A SMALL SAUCEPAN AND BRING IT TO A BUBBLE OVER MEDIUM HEAT.

LOVER B. SWIRL IN THE CORNSTARCH MIXTURE, AND CONTINUE TO STIR FOR 2 MINUTES OR UNTIL THE MARINADE/SAUCE IS THICKENED AND SYRUPY.

LOVERS A AND B. COAT THE RACK OF A BAKING PAN WITH COOKING SPRAY. TAKE TURNS PLACING THE CHICKEN THIGHS ON THE RACK AND SPRINKLE WITH SALT AND PEPPER. BAKE AT 425∞ FOR 30-40 MINUTES, BASTING WITH RESERVED MARINADE EVERY 10 MINUTES.

LOVENOTE: THE CHICKEN THIGHS WILL BE JUICY AND STICKY TO THE TOUCH, BUT THEY ARE DEFINITELY MEANT TO BE EATEN WITH YOUR FINGERS.

AVOCADO AND PINEAPPLE SALAD

SERVES 2

INGREDIENTS

THE SALAD:
8 CUPS CRISP ICEBERG OR ROMAINE LETTUCE
2 CUPS FRESH PINEAPPLE CHUNKS
1 RED ONION, THINLY SLICED

THE DRESSING:
1/3 CUP WHITE VINEGAR
1/3 CUP FRESH ORANGE JUICE
1/4 CUP SUGAR
3/4 TEASPOON KOSHER SALT
1/2 TEASPOON FRESHLY GROUND BLACK PEPPER
1/3 CUP EXTRA-VIRGIN OLIVE OIL

LAGNIAPPE:
2 MEDIUM AVOCADOS, SLICED
FRESH LIME WEDGES

DIRECTIONS

LOVER A. TOSS THE LETTUCE, PINEAPPLE CHUNKS AND ONION SLICES IN A LARGE BOWL.

LOVER B. MAKE THE DRESSING IN A SMALL BOWL, WHISKING TOGETHER THE VINEGAR, ORANGE JUICE, SUGAR, SALT AND PEPPER. KEEP WHISKING AS...

LOVER A. ...DRIZZLES IN THE OLIVE OIL.

LOVER B. POUR DESIRED AMOUNT OF DRESSING OVER SALAD MIXTURE, AND TOSS VERY WELL.

LOVER A. USE TONGS TO TRANSFER THE SALAD ONTO A LARGE PLATE. ARRANGE AVOCADO SLICES OVER THE TOP AND ADD LIME WEDGES.

OYSTERS CHESAPEAKE

SERVES 2

YOU KNOW WHAT THEY SAY ABOUT OYSTERS AND LOVERS, SO BE FOREWARNED.

INGREDIENTS

2 TABLESPOONS MAYONNAISE

2 TABLESPOONS SOUR CREAM

½ TEASPOON WORCESTERSHIRE SAUCE

1 TABLESPOON MINCED CHIVES

1/8 TEASPOON KOSHER SALT

1/8 TEASPOON FRESHLY GROUND BLACK PEPPER

2 BACON SLICES, WELL-COOKED AND CRUMBLED

1 (6 1/2-OUNCE) CAN LUMP CRABMEAT, WITH ITS LIQUID

1 TABLESPOON PANKO BREAD CRUMBS, PLUS MORE FOR SPRINKLING

1 TEASPOON BUTTER, MELTED

12 LARGE SHUCKED OYSTERS

LEMON WEDGES

FRESH MINCED CHIVES FOR GARNISH

DIRECTIONS

LOVER A. GET YOUR BROILER GOOD AND HOT.

LOVER B. IN A MEDIUM BOWL COMBINE THE MAYONNAISE, SOUR CREAM, WORCESTERSHIRE SAUCE, CHIVES, SALT, PEPPER, BACON AND CRABMEAT WITH ITS LIQUID. STIR GENTLY AFTER ADDING EACH INGREDIENT TO THOROUGHLY MINGLE ALL THE INGREDIENTS. STIR IN THE BREAD CRUMBS AND BUTTER.

LOVER A. ARRANGE OYSTERS ON BROILER PAN.

LOVER B. SPOON ABOUT 1 TABLESPOON CRAB MIXTURE OVER EACH OYSTER.

LOVER A. SPRINKLE THE TOP OF EACH WITH MORE BREAD CRUMBS. BROIL 7 MINUTES OR UNTIL TOPS ARE BROWNED. SERVE WITH LEMON WEDGES AND GARNISH WITH CHIVES.

LOVERS A. AND B. WHILE THE OYSTERS ARE BROILING, UNCORK A BOTTLE OF COLD WHITE WINE. POUR SOME WINE INTO TWO GLASSES. ENJOY, ALTERNATING BITES OF OYSTER WITH SIPS OF WINE.

SPICY STRAWBERRY SALSA

SERVES 2

YOU BOTH MIGHT FALL IN LOVE WITH THIS HOT AND
FRUITY PARTNER FOR GRILLED CHICKEN, PORK OR STEAK.

INGREDIENTS

2 TABLESPOON OLIVE OIL

2 TABLESPOON LIME JUICE

2 TABLESPOON RICE WINE VINEGAR

2 1/2 TABLESPOON FRESH MINT LEAVES, CHOPPED

2 1/2 TABLESPOON CILANTRO, CHOPPED

1 JALAPEÑO PEPPER, SEEDED AND MINCED

1/4 TEASPOON KOSHER SALT

1 PINT STRAWBERRIES, HULLED AND CHOPPED

3/4 CUP FRESH PINEAPPLE, DICED AND PEELED

1/2 CUP SWEET ONION, CHOPPED

DIRECTIONS

LOVER A. COMBINE OIL, LIME JUICE, VINEGAR, MINT, CILANTRO, JALAPEÑO PEPPER, AND SALT IN A MIXING BOWL.

LOVER B. TOSS IN THE STRAWBERRIES, PINEAPPLE AND ONION AND MIX IT ALL UP.

LOVENOTE: THE MARRIAGE OF FLAVORS IS DYNAMITE! PUCKER UP AND GET READY FOR A TASTE SENSATION!

SUNDRIED TOMATO AND GOAT CHEESE CROSTINI

SERVES 2

INGREDIENTS

1/2 CUP DRAINED SUN-DRIED TOMATOES IN OIL
1/4 CUP PACKED BASIL LEAVES, PLUS MORE FOR GARNISH
1/4 CUP GRATED PARMESAN
2 GARLIC CLOVES, SMASHED, PLUS 1 WHOLE CLOVE, HALVED
1/4 LEMON, JUICED
1/4 CUP EXTRA-VIRGIN OLIVE OIL
KOSHER SALT AND FRESHLY GROUND BLACK PEPPER
1/4 CUP GOAT CHEESE, AT ROOM TEMPERATURE
1/2 BAGUETTE, SLICED ½-INCH THICK, ON A BIAS

DIRECTIONS

LOVER A. PREHEAT THE BROILER. IN THE BOWL OF A FOOD PROCESSOR COMBINE THE SUN-DRIED TOMATOES, BASIL LEAVES, PARMESAN, SMASHED GARLIC CLOVES AND LEMON JUICE. ADD HALF THE OLIVE OIL AND PURÉE UNTIL SMOOTH. IF THE MIXTURE SEEMS TOO THICK ADD MORE OLIVE OIL. TASTE AND ADJUST SEASONING WITH SALT AND PEPPER.

LOVER B. PLACE THE BAGUETTE SLICES ON A BAKING SHEET AND TOAST THEM IN THE OVEN UNTIL GOLDEN BROWN. RUB EACH SLICE WITH THE CUT SIDES OF THE HALVED GARLIC CLOVE.

LOVER A. SPREAD THE TOASTS WITH THE SOFTENED GOAT CHEESE, TOP EACH WITH A TEASPOONFUL OF SUN-DRIED TOMATO MIXTURE, AND GARNISH WITH THE REMAINING BASIL.

LOVENOTE: THESE MAY BE A BIT MESSY TO EAT, BUT THAT COULD BE PART OF THE FUN.

TUNA AND AVOCADO CEVICHE

SERVES 2

THE SOUTH AMERICAN VERSION OF SUSHI, SORT OF. PERFECT FOR A SOFT SUMMER EVENING OUT ON THE PORCH.
ALTHOUGH THE FISH IS RAW, IT IS COOKED BY THE LIME JUICE.

INGREDIENTS

1/2 POUND SUSHI-GRADE TUNA, SLICED 1/4 INCH THICK AND THEN CUBED
1/2 SMALL RED ONION, HALVED AND THINLY SLICED
1/3 CUP FRESH LIME JUICE
½ TEASPOON SEEDED AND MINCED JALAPEÑO PEPPER
½ TEASPOON SEA SALT
1 LARGE HASS AVOCADO, CUT INTO 1/3-INCH DICE
1/4 CUP COARSELY CHOPPED CILANTRO, PLUS LEAVES FOR GARNISH
SPLASH OF TEQUILA

DIRECTIONS

LOVER A. PLACE THE TUNA IN A MEDIUM MIXING BOWL AND STIR IN THE RED ONION, LIME JUICE, AND JALAPEÑO. COVER THE BOWL WITH PLASTIC WRAP AND REFRIGERATE FOR 1 HOUR, STIRRING GENTLY WITH A RUBBER SPATULA EVERY 15 TO 20 MINUTES

LOVER B. JUST BEFORE SERVING, GENTLY FOLD IN THE SEA SALT, AVOCADO AND CILANTRO. FINISH WITH A TINY SPLASH OF TEQUILA. GARNISH WITH EXTRA CILANTRO AND SERVE WITH ICED PREMIUM-GRADE TEQUILA (DON'T FORGET THE SALT AND THE LIME).

LOVENOTE: IF YOU PREFER, A MARGARITA WOULD PAIR HAPPILY WITH THE CEVICHE.

TRUFFLE PARMESAN POPCORN

SERVES 2

SEXY MAGIC WITH TRUFFLE OIL. NOTHING TASTES QUITE LIKE IT,
AND YOU'LL NEVER EAT MOVIE POPCORN AGAIN.

INGREDIENTS

1/2 CUP UNSALTED BUTTER
1/4 CUP CHOPPED FRESH CHIVES
2 TEASPOONS BLACK TRUFFLE SALT
2 TEASPOONS WHITE TRUFFLE OIL
FRESHLY GROUND BLACK PEPPER, TO TASTE
1 BAG MICROWAVE ALL NATURAL POPCORN, POPPED AS DIRECTED
1 CUP GRATED PARMESAN

DIRECTIONS

LOVER A. MELT THE BUTTER IN A SMALL SAUCEPAN OVER MEDIUM HEAT. AND CHIVES AND SAUTÉ FOR A FEW SECONDS OVER MEDIUM HEAT. REMOVE FROM THE HEAT. ADD THE TRUFFLE SALT AND TRUFFLE OIL, AND SEASON WITH BLACK PEPPER.

LOVER B. POUR THE POPCORN INTO A LARGE BOWL, DRIZZLE WITH THE TRUFFLE BUTTER AND SPRINKLE WITH PARMESAN.

LOVENOTE: KEEP THE BOWL BETWEEN YOU AS YOU WATCH A ROMANTIC MOVIE. LICK FINGERS OFTEN.

LOBSTER EGGS BENEDICT

SERVES 2

INGREDIENTS

1 FEMALE LOBSTER, COOKED AND SHELLED, ROE REMOVED AND RESERVED

HOLLANDAISE SAUCE:
1/2 STICK UNSALTED BUTTER, SLICED
4 EGG YOLKS
½ STICK UNSALTED BUTTER, MELTED
1 TEASPOON DIJON MUSTARD
1 SPLASH HOT SAUCE
RESERVED LOBSTER ROE
1 LEMON, JUICED

1 TABLESPOON UNSALTED BUTTER
4 SLICES CANADIAN BACON
2 ENGLISH MUFFINS, SPLIT
4 EGGS
MINCED FRESH PARSLEY
PAPRIKA

DIRECTIONS

LOVER A. MELT THE HALF STICK OF SLICED BUTTER IN A HEAT-PROOF BOWL SET OVER A POT OF SIMMERING (NOT BOILING) WATER. IN A MEDIUM BOWL WHISK THE EGG YOLKS AND WHISK THEM INTO THE MELTED BUTTER. WHISK IN THE MELTED HALF STICK OF BUTTER, KEEPING THE HEAT LOW UNDER THE POT. STIR IN THE MUSTARD AND HOT SAUCE AND CONTINUE TO WHISK UNTIL A RIBBON FORMS WHEN THE WHISK IS LIFTED.

LOVER B. CRUMBLE THE LOBSTER ROE AS FINELY AS POSSIBLE AND STIR IT INTO THE SAUCE. SLOWLY STREAM IN THE LEMON JUICE AND WHISK TO INCORPORATE. SET ASIDE AND KEEP WARM.

LOVER A. DICE THE COOKED LOBSTER MEAT. MELT THE REMAINING 1 TABLESPOON BUTTER IN A SKILLET OVER MEDIUM HEAT. ADD THE DICED LOBSTER AND SAUTÉ JUST LONG ENOUGH TO HEAT THROUGH. REMOVE THE LOBSTER MEAT TO A BOWL AND KEEP WARM.

LOVER B. BROWN THE CANADIAN BACON IN THE SAME SKILLET, TURN OFF THE HEAT AND KEEP WARM. TOAST THE SPLIT ENGLISH MUFFINS.

LOVER A. POACH THE EGGS IN A PAN OF SIMMERING WATER WITH A TABLESPOON OF VINEGAR AND A DASH OF SALT ADDED. THEY SHOULD SIMMER FOR 3 TO 4 MINUTES OR UNTIL THE WHITES ARE JUST FIRM.

LOVER B. PLACE TWO TOASTED MUFFIN HALVES, SPLIT-SIDE UP, ON EACH PLATE AND CAREFULLY LAYER ON THE LOBSTER MEAT, CANADIAN BACON SLICES, AND POACHED EGGS. COVER WITH HOLLANDAISE SAUCE AND GARNISH WITH THE PARSLEY AND PAPRIKA.

SWEET & SPICY EDAMAME

SERVES 2

SWEETNESS AND SPICE ARE BRILLIANT TOGETHER.

INGREDIENTS

2 CUPS FROZEN EDAMAME IN THEIR SHELL

1 TEASPOON CANOLA OIL

1 TEASPOON GARLIC, MINCED

1/2 TEASPOON MINCED FRESH GINGER

2 TABLESPOONS LIGHT SOY SAUCE

2 TABLESPOONS WATER

1 TABLESPOON RICE VINEGAR

1/4 CUP BROWN SUGAR

1/2 TEASPOON CRUSHED RED PEPPER FLAKES

DIRECTIONS

LOVER A. COOK THE EDAMAME ACCORDING TO PACKAGE DIRECTIONS, DRAIN AND PLACE IN A SERVING BOWL.

LOVER B. HEAT THE OIL IN A SMALL SAUCEPAN OVER MEDIUM-LOW HEAT. ADD THE GARLIC AND GINGER AND SAUTÉ 1 TO 2 MINUTES, STIRRING FREQUENTLY.

LOVER A. IN A SMALL BOWL COMBINE THE SOY SAUCE, WATER, RICE VINEGAR, BROWN SUGAR AND RED PEPPER FLAKES. STIR THIS MIXTURE INTO THE SAUCEPAN AND THE GARLIC-GINGER MIXTURE. RAISE THE HEAT TO MEDIUM-HIGH AND COOK, STIRRING FREQUENTLY, UNTIL THE SAUCE REDUCES TO A GLAZE, ABOUT 6 TO 7 MINUTES. POUR OVER THE COOKED EDAMAME AND TOSS WELL.

TOASTED BAGUETTE WITH DARK CHOCOLATE AND SALT

SERVES 2

BREAD AND CHOCOLATE, A PRIMITIVE PAIRING NOT TO BE MISSED.

INGREDIENTS

½ BAGUETTE, SLICED IN HALF
1 TEASPOON UNSALTED BUTTER, ROOM TEMPERATURE
1 DARK CHOCOLATE BAR
MALDON SEA SALT

DIRECTIONS

LOVER A. PREHEAT OVEN TO 350. SPREAD BUTTER ON ONE HALF OF THE BAGUETTE. PLACE BOTH HALVES ON A BAKING SHEET, SLIDE INTO THE OVEN AND BAKE UNTIL GOLDEN, ABOUT 4 TO 5 MINUTES.

LOVER B. REMOVE FROM THE OVEN AND PLACE THE CHOCOLATE BAR IMMEDIATELY ON THE BREAD. SPRINKLE LIGHTLY WITH SALT. TOP WITH THE OTHER HALF, PRESSING THE TOAST HALVES TOGETHER WHILE HOT TO MELT THE CHOCOLATE.

LOVENOTE: MORE SOPHISTICATED THAN S'MORES, AND LOTS MORE SEXY.

FORBIDDEN LOVE

SERVES 2

SPECIAL EQUIPMENT: COCKTAIL SHAKER, STRAINER, 2 MARTINI GLASSES

INGREDIENTS

4 FRESH RIPE STRAWBERRIES, SLICED
DASH SIMPLE SYRUP
4 OUNCES HENDRICKS GIN
2 OUNCES BLOOD ORANGE JUICE
THIN SPIRAL OF CUCUMBER
ORANGE PEEL

DIRECTIONS

LOVER A. MUDDLE THE STRAWBERRIES WITH SIMPLE SYRUP, ADD GIN AND BLOOD ORANGE JUICE.

LOVER B. SHAKE AND STRAIN INTO A MARTINI GLASS. GARNISH WITH CUCUMBER SPIRAL AND ORANGE PEEL.

LOVENOTE: FORBIDDEN, BUT NEVER FORSAKEN.

BAKED BRIE WITH HONEY

SERVES 2

OH, TASTES AND TEXTURES OF THIS "LOVERS' FAVORITE."

INGREDIENTS

1 8OZ WHEEL BRIE
1/2 CUP SHELLED PISTACHIOS
1/2 CUP HONEY
1/4 CUP ROUGHLY CHOPPED DRIED CRANBERRIES
CRACKERS OR CROSTINI FOR SERVING

DIRECTIONS

LOVER A. HEAT OVEN TO 350 DEGREES AND ARRANGE A RACK IN THE MIDDLE. DECANT A BOTTLE OF MERLOT OR PINOT NOIR.

LOVER B. PLACE THE BRIE IN A SMALL OVENPROOF BAKING DISH AND BAKE UNTIL STILL INTACT BUT CHEESE IS SOFT AND SLIGHTLY MELTED, ABOUT 15 TO 20 MINUTES. SET ASIDE TO COOL SLIGHTLY, ABOUT 10 MINUTES.

LOVER A. WHILE THE BRIE IS COOLING, BAKE THE PISTACHIOS ON A COOKIE SHEET OR IN A SMALL PAN IN THE OVEN UNTIL GOLDEN BROWN AND TOASTED, ABOUT 10 MINUTES, WHILE...

LOVER B. ...HEATS THE HONEY IN A SMALL SAUCEPAN OVER MEDIUM HEAT. WHEN THE HONEY COMES TO A BUBBLE, REMOVE THE SAUCEPAN FROM THE BURNER.

LOVER A. PLACE THE CHEESE ON A SERVING PLATE, TOP WITH A FEW SPOONSFUL OF THE HONEY, THE TOASTED PISTACHIOS AND DRIED CRANBERRIES. SERVE IMMEDIATELY WITH CRACKERS AND GLASSES OF MERLOT OR PINOT NOIR.

SMOKED SALMON
CREAM CHEESE AND CHIVE OMELETTE

SERVES 2

HERE'S A LOVELY WAY TO TIPTOE INTO SUNDAY...

INGREDIENTS

8 EGGS
1/4 CUP HEAVY CREAM
2 TABLESPOON UNSALTED BUTTER
1/4 POUND SMOKED SALMON, CHOPPED
1 CUP CREAM CHEESE, ROOM TEMPERATURE
6 GREEN ONIONS, THINLY SLICED
KOSHER SALT AND FRESHLY GROUND BLACK PEPPER

DIRECTIONS

LOVER A. WHISK THE EGGS AND HEAVY CREAM TOGETHER IN A LARGE MIXING BOWL. START PREPARING THE BESTEVER BLOODY MARY, PAGE 108.

LOVER B. PLACE THE BUTTER IN A LARGE NONSTICK PAN OVER MEDIUM HEAT, TIPPING THE PAN TO MAKE SURE IT'S COVERED EVENLY. ONCE THE BUTTER STARTS TO FOAM TURN THE HEAT DOWN TO MEDIUM-LOW AND ADD THE EGGS. USING A SPATULA SWIRL THE EGGS QUICKLY IN A CIRCULAR MOTION AS YOU GENTLY SHAKE THE PAN BACK AND FORTH.

LOVER A. ONCE THE EGGS BEGIN TO SET, DROP PIECES OF SALMON, SMALL SPOONSFUL OF CREAM CHEESE AND GREEN ONIONS OVER THE TOP. SEASON WITH SALT AND PEPPER.

LOVER B. SLIDE IT OUT ONTO YOUR CUTTING BOARD AND FOLD ONE SIDE OVER THE OTHER AS TO FORM AN OMELETTE.

LOVENOTE: GRAB THE SUNDAY PAPERS AND A PLATEFUL OF OMELETTE AND TIPTOE BACK TO BED. AND DON'T FORGET THE BLOODY MARYS!

PARISIAN
MUSSLES

SERVES 2

THIS SIMPLE DISH WILL WIN YOUR HEART, AND YOU MIGHT EVEN FIND YOURSELVES LICKING THE PLATE...
IF NO ONE'S WATCHING. BET IT WILL BECOME PART OF YOUR REPERTOIRE.

INGREDIENTS

3 TABLESPOONS EXTRA-VIRGIN OLIVE OIL

3 SHALLOTS, MINCED

5 GARLIC CLOVES, MINCED

1 POUND MUSSELS, CLEANED AND DE-BEARDED

1 CUP DRY WHITE WINE

1/2 CUP HEAVY CREAM

4 TABLESPOONS UNSALTED BUTTER, CUT INTO PIECES

1/2 BUNCH FRESH PARSLEY, CHOPPED

KOSHER SALT AND FRESHLY GROUND BLACK PEPPER

CRUSTY BREAD, TO SERVE

DIRECTIONS

LOVER A. HEAT THE OIL IN A LARGE POT OVER MEDIUM-HIGH HEAT. ADD THE SHALLOTS AND GARLIC AND SAUTÉ UNTIL SOFTENED, STIRRING OCCASIONALLY, ABOUT 5 TO 7 MINUTES.

LOVER B. ADD THE MUSSELS, WINE, CREAM, BUTTER, AND PARSLEY AND SEASON WITH SALT AND PEPPER. COVER THE POT, AND COOK JUST UNTIL THE MUSSELS OPEN AND ARE COOKED THROUGH, ABOUT 10 TO 12 MINUTES.

LOVENOTE: DO AS THE FRENCH DO -- ENJOY WITH CRUSTY BREAD AND A BOTTLE OF CHILLED WHITE.

WALNUT AND GREEN APPLE SALAD WITH GOAT CHEESE TOAST

SERVES 2

INGREDIENTS

1 TABLESPOON WHITE WINE VINEGAR

1 TABLESPOON SHALLOTS, MINCED

1 TEASPOON DIJON MUSTARD

1/4 TEASPOON KOSHER SALT

FRESHLY GROUND PEPPER, TO TASTE

3 TABLESPOONS EXTRA-VIRGIN OLIVE OIL

1 BAGUETTE, CUT INTO 1/2-INCH SLICES

3 CUPS FRISÉE LETTUCE

1 CUP WALNUT HALVES, TOASTED

1 GRANNY SMITH APPLE, THINLY SLICED

KOSHER SALT AND FRESHLY GROUND PEPPER, TO TASTE

6 OUNCES MILD GOAT CHEESE, CUT INTO ¼ INCH MEDALLION SLICES

EXTRA-VIRGIN OLIVE OIL, FOR DRIZZLING

DIRECTIONS

LOVER A. PREHEAT THE OVEN TO 350 DEGREES. TO PREPARE THE DRESSING COMBINE THE VINEGAR, SHALLOT, MUSTARD, SALT AND PEPPER IN A BOWL. ADD THE OIL IN A SLOW STREAM, WHISKING UNTIL EMULSIFIED.

LOVER B. PLACE BAGUETTE SLICES ON A BAKING SHEET, AND TOAST UNTIL GOLDEN, ABOUT 8 TO 10 MINUTES. REMOVE THE BREAD AND TURN THE OVEN HEAT TO BROIL. MEANWHILE, TOSS TOGETHER THE FRISÉE, WALNUTS AND APPLE SLICES IN A LARGE BOWL.

LOVER A. ADD THE DRESSING TO THE SALAD MIXTURE, AND TOSS TO COAT EVENLY. SEASON WITH SALT AND PEPPER. TRANSFER TO A SERVING PLATE.

LOVER B. PLACE THE CHEESE ON A BAKING SHEET AND DRIZZLE WITH OIL. BROIL UNTIL TOP IS BROWNED AND BUBBLING, ABOUT 4 MINUTES. SERVE WITH THE BAGUETTE TOASTS AND SALAD.

HOT CANDIED
BACON

SERVES 2

AS A SNACK, A SIDE DISH OR EVEN DESSERT, THIS TREAT IS LIP-LICKING LUSCIOUS!

INGREDIENTS

1 CUP PACKED LIGHT BROWN SUGAR
3/4 TEASPOON CAYENNE PEPPER
1/2 POUND THICKLY SLICED BACON

DIRECTIONS

LOVER A. PREHEAT THE OVEN TO 350 DEGREES. WHILE IT IS HEATING, LINE A BAKING SHEET WITH ALUMINUM FOIL. COMBINE THE BROWN SUGAR AND CAYENNE IN A SHALLOW DISH, STIRRING TO MIX WELL.

LOVER B. PRESS 1 SIDE OF EACH SLICE OF BACON FIRMLY INTO THE SPICED SUGAR TO COAT. ARRANGE THE SLICES OF BACON, SUGARED SIDE UP, ON THE BAKING SHEET IN A SINGLE LAYER. IF THERE IS ANY SUGAR REMAINING IN THE DISH, SPRINKLE IT EVENLY OVER THE BACON SLICES.

LOVER A. BAKE UNTIL THE BACON IS CRISP AND THE SUGAR IS BUBBLY, 15 TO 20 MINUTES. REMOVE FROM THE OVEN AND ALLOW THE BACON TO COOL FOR 10-12 MINUTES BEFORE SERVING.

CANDIED
ALMONDS

SERVES 2

A STICKY TREAT TO BE ENJOYED AT ANY TIME OF THE DAY OR NIGHT.

INGREDIENTS

1 CUP SUGAR

1 TABLESPOON GROUND CINNAMON

1/4 TEASPOON KOSHER SALT

1/2 CUP WATER

2 CUPS WHOLE ALMONDS

DIRECTIONS

LOVER A. COMBINE THE SUGAR, CINNAMON, SALT AND WATER IN A SAUCEPAN OVER MEDIUM HEAT AND BRING TO A BOIL. ADD THE ALMONDS AND COOK, STIRRING, UNTIL THE LIQUID EVAPORATES AND LEAVES A SYRUP-LIKE COATING ON THE ALMONDS.

LOVER B. POUR THE ALMONDS ONTO A BAKING SHEET LINED WITH WAXED PAPER AND SEPARATE THE NUTS WITH A FORK.

LOVERS A. AND B. SIP A GLASS OF CHILLED WINE WHILE WAITING FOR THE ALMONDS TO COOL, ABOUT 20 MINUTES. DIG IN.

GRILLED STEAK & PEACH SALAD

SERVES 2

SPECIAL EQUIPMENT: A SKILLET-GRILL: A NON-STICK SKILLET WITH RAISED GRILL RIDGES.

INGREDIENTS

FOR THE STEAK:
1 1/4 CUPS EXTRA-VIRGIN OLIVE OIL
2 GARLIC CLOVES, SMASHED
1 12 -OUNCE NEW YORK STRIP STEAK
KOSHER SALT AND FRESHLY GROUND BLACK PEPPER

FOR THE DRESSING:
1/4 POUND BLUE CHEESE, CRUMBLED
1/4 CUP SOUR CREAM
1 TABLESPOON FRESH LEMON JUICE
1 TABLESPOON RED WINE VINEGAR
PINCH OF CAYENNE PEPPER
2 TEASPOONS MINCED FRESH CHIVES

FOR THE SALAD:
2 PEACHES, HALVED AND PITTED
4 CUPS MESCLUN GREENS
2 TABLESPOONS CHOPPED FRESH CHIVES
3 TABLESPOONS THINLY SLICED FRESH BASIL
FRESHLY GROUND BLACK PEPPER

DIRECTIONS

LOVER A. HEAT THE OLIVE OIL AND GARLIC IN A SMALL SAUCEPAN OVER LOW HEAT, UNTIL THE GARLIC IS LIGHTLY BROWNED. REMOVE FROM THE HEAT AND LET COOL TO ROOM TEMPERATURE.

LOVER B. PAT THE STEAK DRY, SEASON WITH SALT AND BLACK PEPPER AND PLACE IN A SHALLOW PAN. POUR 1 CUP OF THE GARLIC-INFUSED OIL OVER THE STEAK, COVER AND REFRIGERATE FOR 3 HOURS. REMOVE FROM THE REFRIGERATOR ABOUT 45 MINUTES BEFORE COOKING.

LOVER A. HEAT A DRY SKILLET-GRILL OVER MEDIUM-HIGH HEAT UNTIL VERY HOT. SEASON THE STEAK WITH SALT AND BLACK PEPPER AND GRILL 5 TO 6 MINUTES PER SIDE FOR MEDIUM RARE. REMOVE TO A CUTTING BOARD AND LET REST 10 MINUTES BEFORE SLICING.

LOVER B. TO MAKE THE DRESSING, WHISK HALF THE BLUE CHEESE WITH THE SOUR CREAM, LEMON JUICE, VINEGAR AND CAYENNE IN A SMALL BOWL UNTIL SMOOTH. FOLD IN THE CHIVES, COVER AND CHILL.

LOVER A. RE-HEAT THE SKILLET-GRILL OVER MEDIUM-HIGH HEAT. BRUSH THE PEACHES WITH THE REMAINING 1/4 CUP GARLIC-INFUSED OIL. GRILL THE PEACHES, CUT-SIDE DOWN, 4 MINUTES. TURN THEM OVER AND GRILL THE OTHER SIDE 1 TO 2 MINUTES. REMOVE AND SLICE INTO WEDGES.

LOVER B. TOSS THE GREENS AND HERBS IN A LARGE BOWL. ARRANGE THE STEAK SLICES AND PEACH WEDGES ON TOP OF THE GREENS. DRIZZLE WITH THE DRESSING AND TOP WITH THE REMAINING BLUE CHEESE.

ROASTED GARLIC FINGERLING POTATOES

SERVES 2

INGREDIENTS

1/2 POUND FINGERLING POTATOES

1/4 CUP EXTRA VIRGIN OLIVE OIL

8 GARLIC CLOVES, SLICED

1 TABLESPOON FRESHLY CHOPPED ITALIAN PARSLEY LEAVES

KOSHER SALT AND FRESHLY GROUND BLACK PEPPER

DIRECTIONS

LOVER A. HEAT THE OVEN TO 350 DEGREES WHILE YOU WATCH...

LOVER B. ...ARRANGE AN ARMLOAD OF WILDFLOWERS IN A LARGE VASE.

LOVER A. IN A SMALL BAKING DISH COMBINE THE POTATOES, OIL, GARLIC, PARSLEY, SALT AND PEPPER. ROAST FOR 25 MINUTES OR UNTIL THE POTATOES ARE TENDER AND THE FLOWERS ARE PERFUMING THE AIR.

CUCUMBER AND CHERRY PEPPER SALAD

SERVES 2

INGREDIENTS

1 CUCUMBER, PEELED

1/2 TEASPOON KOSHER SALT

1 TABLESPOON MINCED RED ONION

1/4 CUP SOUR CREAM

1 TEASPOON SUGAR

1/4 CUP THINLY SLICED PICKLED CHERRY PEPPERS

DIRECTIONS

LOVER A. CUT THE CUCUMBER IN 1/4 –THICK SLICES AND TOSS IN A BOWL WITH THE SALT. ALLOW TO SIT FOR AT LEAST 1 HOUR. PAT DRY AND WIPE OFF MOISTURE AND EXCESS SALT WITH A PAPER TOWEL.

LOVER B. IN A MIXING BOWL COMBINE THE ONION WITH THE SOUR CREAM, SUGAR AND CHERRY PEPPERS. ADD THE CUCUMBERS AND TOSS LIGHTLY.

MANGO
TARTE TATIN

SERVES 2

HERE'S ANOTHER TAKE ON A TARTE TATIN, WHICH IS LIKE AN UPSIDE-DOWN TART.

INGREDIENTS

PASTRY DOUGH TOPPING:
1 1/4 CUPS ALL-PURPOSE FLOUR, PLUS ADDITIONAL FOR ROLLING
1/4 CUP GRANULATED SUGAR
1/2 TEASPOON KOSHER SALT
8 TABLESPOONS (1 STICK) UNSALTED BUTTER, CUBED AND CHILLED
1 EGG YOLK
ICE WATER

TART FILLING:
4 RIPE BUT FIRM MANGOES, PEELED
1 1/2 CUPS GRANULATED SUGAR
4 TABLESPOONS UNSALTED BUTTER

DIRECTIONS

LOVER A. PREHEAT THE OVEN TO 350 DEGREES. IN A FOOD PROCESSOR BLEND THE FLOUR, SUGAR AND SALT. ADD THE BUTTER, 1 TABLESPOON AT A TIME, AND PULSE TO BLEND UNTIL THE MIXTURE IS CRUMBLY. ADD THE YOLK, AND PULSE. ADD ENOUGH ICE WATER, 1 TABLESPOON AT A TIME, UNTIL THE DOUGH ADHERES TO ITSELF.

LOVER B. TURN THE DOUGH ONTO A LIGHTLY FLOURED FLAT SURFACE. KNEAD THE DOUGH UNTIL SMOOTH, FLATTEN IT, WRAP IN PLASTIC AND REFRIGERATE AT LEAST 20 MINUTES.

LOVER A. HOLD EACH MANGO UPRIGHT ON A FLAT SURFACE AND, ONE BY ONE CUT A SLICE OFF EACH SIDE. CUT AS CLOSE AS YOU CAN TO THE PIT TO GET THE MOST FLESH FROM EACH MANGO. SLICE THE SMALLER PIECE OFF THE TOP AND BOTTOM OF EACH FRUIT. CUT THE MANGO SLICES INTO SMALLER PIECES, ABOUT ONE INCH SQUARE.

LOVER B. IN A SAUTÉ PAN OVER MEDIUM-LOW HEAT, MELT THE SUGAR, STIRRING, UNTIL IT BECOMES GOLDEN BROWN. ADD THE BUTTER. REMOVE THE SKILLET FROM THE HEAT AND SPOON EQUAL AMOUNTS OF THE CARAMELIZED SUGAR MIXTURE INTO EACH RAMEKIN. DIVIDE THE MANGO PIECES AMONG THE RAMEKINS AND PRESS THE FRUIT INTO THE CARAMEL SAUCE.

LOVER A. ROLL OUT THE DOUGH ON A FLOURED SURFACE AND USE THE RIM OF A GLASS OR CUP TO CUT OUT CIRCLES SLIGHTLY LARGER THAN THE TOPS OF THE RAMEKINS. TUCK THE DOUGH EDGES INSIDE THE RAMEKINS TO COVER THE FRUIT, ANDCUT A SMALL SLIT IN THE TOP OF EACH.

LOVER B. PLACE THE RAMEKINS ON A SHEET PAN IN THE CENTER OF THE OVEN AND BAKE UNTIL THE PASTRY BROWNS, 15 TO 20 MINUTES. REMOVE THE RAMEKINS FROM THE OVEN AND ALLOW THEM TO COOL FOR 10 MINUTES.

LOVENOTE: THIS DISH IS FOR DEDICATED LOVERCOOKS. AND REMEMBER, ALWAYS SIP WINE WHILE WORKING!

ARUGULA SALAD WITH ROASTED ASPARAGUS

SERVES 2

ROASTING ASPARAGUS BRINGS OUT A DEEP, EARTHY TASTE THAT PAIRS BEAUTIFULLY WITH WINE.

INGREDIENTS

10 FRESH ASPARAGUS SPEARS

2 TABLESPOONS EXTRA VIRGIN OLIVE OIL, IN ALL

1 TABLESPOON BALSAMIC VINEGAR

1 TEASPOON DIJON MUSTARD

1/8 TEASPOON KOSHER SALT

1/8 TEASPOON FRESHLY GROUND BLACK PEPPER

4 CUPS BABY ARUGULA LEAVES

1 TABLESPOON FRESHLY GRATED PARMIGIANO REGGIANO CHEESE

DIRECTIONS

LOVER A. HEAT UP THE OVEN TO 400 DEGREES. SNAP OFF THE TOUGH ENDS OF THE ASPARAGUS.

LOVER B. LINE A BAKING SHEET WITH FOIL. LAY SPEARS IN A SINGLE LAYER ON THE FOIL AND BRUSH THEM WITH ABOUT 1/2 TABLESPOON OF THE OLIVE OIL. SPRINKLE WITH SALT AND PEPPER AND ROAST UNTIL TENDER CRISP AND SLIGHTLY CHARRED, ABOUT 8 TO 10 MINUTES.

LOVER A. WHILE THE ASPARAGUS IS ROASTING, PREPARE THE DRESSING: IN A SMALL BOWL WHISK TOGETHER THE VINEGAR, MUSTARD, SALT AND PEPPER, AND CONTINUE WHISKING WHILE...

LOVER B. ...DRIZZLES IN THE REMAINING OLIVE OIL. AND UNCORKS A COLD BOTTLE OF WHITE WINE.

LOVER A. TOSS THE ARUGULA WITH DRESSING AND ARRANGE ON A LARGE PLATTER. TOP WITH ASPARAGUS SPEARS AND SPRINKLE CHEESE OVER ALL.

LOVER B. POUR THE WINE.

LOVENOTE: THE SALAD IS BEST EATEN WITH FORKS, BUT IF YOU'RE IN THE MOOD, NIBBLE THE ASPARAGUS SPEARS USING YOUR FINGERS.

CHILI LIME SHRIMP

SERVES 2

MMM...THIS IS A MOUTHFUL OF FLAVOR.

INGREDIENTS

1 TABLESPOON CANOLA OIL

3/4 CUP CHOPPED GREEN ONIONS, IN ALL

1 TEASPOON GARLIC, MINCED

1/2 POUND PEELED AND DEVEINED LARGE SHRIMP

1 TEASPOON CHILI POWDER

2 TABLESPOONS FRESHLY-SQUEEZED LIME JUICE

2 TABLESPOONS BUTTER, ROOM TEMPERATURE.

1/2 TEASPOON KOSHER SALT

DIRECTIONS

LOVER A. HEAT THE OIL IN A LARGE SAUTÉ PAN OVER MEDIUM-HIGH HEAT. ADD THE GARLIC AND 1/2 CUP OF THE GREEN ONIONS AND SAUTÉ FOR 1 MINUTE, STIRRING OCCASIONALLY.

LOVER B. ADD THE SHRIMP AND CHILI POWDER AND COOK, TURNING THE SHRIMP ONCE OR TWICE, 4 TO 5 MINUTES OR UNTIL THEY ARE PINK. ADD THE LIME JUICE, BUTTER AND SALT, AND STIR UNTIL THE BUTTER MELTS. SPRINKLE WITH REMAINING 1/4 CUP GREEN ONIONS.

LOVENOTE: CAN YOU SAY MARGARITA? NOW, CAN YOU MAKE A MARGARITA...?

ORANGE BEEF AND BROCCOLI

SERVES 2

INGREDIENTS

1 NAVEL ORANGE
3 TABLESPOONS CORNSTARCH, IN ALL
1 LARGE EGG WHITE
1/2 POUND BEEF SIRLOIN, TRIMMED OF FAT AND CUT INTO 2-INCH SLICES
1/2 BAG BROCCOLI FLORETS
3 TABLESPOONS CANOLA OIL, IN ALL
1/2 CUP CHICKEN BROTH
¼ CUP ASIAN ORANGE SAUCE
1/4 CUP REDUCED-SODIUM SOY SAUCE
1-1/2 TEASPOONS GRATED FRESH GINGER
1-1/2 TEASPOONS GARLIC, MINCED
1/2 TEASPOON CRUSHED RED PEPPER FLAKES
1/2 CUP SHREDDED CARROTS
1 CUP COOKED RICE

DIRECTIONS

LOVER A. REMOVE THE PEEL FROM THE ORANGE USING A VEGETABLE PEELER AND RESERVE. SQUEEZE THE ORANGE AND RESERVE THE JUICE. IN A MEDIUM BOWL, WHISK 1 TABLESPOON OF THE ORANGE JUICE, 2 TABLESPOONS OF THE CORNSTARCH, AND THE EGG WHITE UNTIL BLENDED. ADD THE BEEF STRIPS TO THIS MIXTURE AND TOSS TO COAT.

LOVER B. MICROWAVE THE BROCCOLI WITH 2 TABLESPOONS WATER IN A MICROWAVE-SAFE BOWL COVERED WITH VENTED PLASTIC WRAP, 2 TO 3 MINUTES ON HIGH, OR UNTIL TENDER. DRAIN; REFRESH UNDER COLD WATER AND SET ASIDE.

LOVER A. IN A SMALL BOWL COMBINE THE REMAINING ORANGE JUICE AND CORNSTARCH, THE BROTH, ORANGE SAUCE, SOY SAUCE, GINGER AND GARLIC.

LOVER B. DRAIN THE BEEF AND HEAT 2 TABLESPOONS OF THE OIL IN A LARGE, DEEP NONSTICK SAUTÉ PAN OVER MEDIUM-HIGH HEAT. COOK THE BEEF IN TWO BATCHES, 1 TO 2 MINUTES PER SIDE UNTIL GOLDEN BROWN, AND SET THE PIECES ON PAPER TOWELS.

LOVER A. ADD THE REMAINING OIL TO THE PAN. ADD THE ORANGE PEEL AND PEPPER FLAKES AND COOK FOR 2 TO 3 MINUTES, OR UNTIL THE PEEL BEGINS TO DARKEN AND SMELL FRAGRANT. POUR THE RESERVED ORANGE SAUCE MIXTURE INTO THE SKILLET AND COOK, STIRRING, UNTIL BUBBLY AND SAUCE STARTS TO THICKEN.

LOVER B. ADD BROCCOLI, BEEF, AND CARROT AND CONTINUE TO COOK 2 TO 3 MINUTES, STIRRING, UNTIL HOT AND COATED WITH SAUCE. SERVE OVER COOKED RICE.

LOVENOTE. THE COMBINATION OF THE SWEET CITRUS AND THE HOT SPICINESS OF THIS DISH GETS THE BLOOD PUMPING!

EXTRADIRTY
MARTINI

SERVES 2

PSST...LOVER A. HERE'S A WAY TO WARM YOUR LOVER'S HEART. MAKE IT A SURPRISE GIFT FROM YOU.

INGREDIENTS

4 OUNCES GOOD-QUALITY VODKA
4 TEASPOONS GREEN OLIVE BRINE
1 OUNCE VERMOUTH
OLIVES FOR GARNISH

DIRECTIONS

LOVER A. FILL A COCKTAIL SHAKER WITH ICE. ADD THE VODKA, OLIVE BRINE, AND VERMOUTH; SHAKE VIGOROUSLY. STRAIN INTO TWO CHILLED MARTINI GLASSES. GARNISH WITH GREEN OLIVES.

LOVER A. SURPRISE LOVER B WITH THIS EXTRA DIRTY MARTINI. JAMES BOND WOULD BE PROUD OF YOU!

BLUEBERRY BUTTERMILK PANCAKES WITH BOURBON MAPLE SYRUP

SERVES 2

A TREAT FOR A LAZY MORNING. OR A LAZY LATE-NIGHT.

INGREDIENTS

2 CUPS ALL-PURPOSE FLOUR

1/3 CUP SUGAR

2 TEASPOONS BAKING POWDER

1/2 TEASPOON BAKING SODA

1/2 TEASPOON KOSHER SALT

2 EGGS

2 CUPS BUTTERMILK

1/4 CUP MELTED UNSALTED BUTTER

1 CUP FRESH RIPE BLUEBERRIES

1/4 CUP BOURBON WHISKEY

1 CUP PURE MAPLE SYRUP

DIRECTIONS

LOVER A. IN A LARGE BOWL SIFT TOGETHER THE FLOUR, SUGAR, BAKING POWDER, BAKING SODA AND SALT.

LOVER B. BEAT THE EGGS WITH THE BUTTERMILK AND MELTED BUTTER. COMBINE THE WET AND DRY INGREDIENTS AND WHISK OR STIR INTO A LUMPY BATTER. DO NOT OVER-BEAT OR THE MIXTURE WILL BECOME TOUGH.

LOVER A. HEAT THE BUTTER IN A LARGE PAN OVER MEDIUM HEAT UNTIL IT SIZZLES. SPOON 1/3 CUP OF THE BATTER INTO THE PAN AND SPRINKLE THE TOP WITH SOME OF THE BLUEBERRIES. COOK FOR 2 TO 3 MINUTES ON EACH SIDE UNTIL THE EDGES BUBBLE, THEN FLIP AND REPEAT TWICE WHILE...

LOVER B. ...COMBINES THE BOURBON AND MAPLE SYRUP IN A SMALL SAUCEPAN AND BRINGS IT TO A QUICK BOIL. REMOVES IT FROM THE HEAT AND DRIBBLES IT OVER THE PANCAKES.

LOVENOTE: SHARE THE STACK OF PANCAKES, PERHAPS FEEDING ONE ANOTHER...

HONEY TRUFFLE CROQUE-AMORE

SERVES 2

SOME OF THE SIMPLEST PLEASURES ARE OFTEN THE SEXIEST.

INGREDIENTS

2 THICK SLICES BRIOCHE OR CHALLAH
4 SLICES GRUYERE CHEESE
HONEY
1/2 TEASPOON WHITE TRUFFLE OIL
1/4 CUP BUTTER, SOFTENED

DIRECTIONS

LOVER A. LAY OUT THE BREAD. COVER ONE PIECE WITH CHEESE SLICES. DRIZZLE WITH A LITTLE HONEY AND TRUFFLE OIL. COVER WITH THE OTHER SLICE OF BREAD. SPREAD THE BUTTER ON BOTH SIDES OF THE SANDWICH.

LOVER B. MEANWHILE, PLACE A NON-STICK SKILLET OVER MEDIUM HEAT. WHEN THE PAN IS HOT, ADD THE SANDWICH AND COOK UNTIL GOLDEN BROWN ON ONE SIDE. FLIP OVER AND COOK THE OTHER SIDE UNTIL THE BREAD IS GOLDEN BROWN AND THE CHEESE IS OOZING FROM THE SIDES. CUT IN HALF AND ENJOY.

CORN AND QUESO
BREAKFAST BURRITO

SERVES 2

INGREDIENTS

2 TABLESPOONS EXTRA-VIRGIN OLIVE OIL
1/4 CUP MINCED GREEN BELL PEPPER
1/4 CUP MINCED RED BELL PEPPER
1/4 CUP MINCED YELLOW ONION
1 CUP FRESH CORN KERNELS
1/2 JALAPEÑO, MINCED
2 TEASPOONS MINCED GARLIC
1 TEASPOON KOSHER SALT, DIVIDED
4 LARGE EGGS
2 TABLESPOONS HEAVY CREAM
1/4 TEASPOON FRESHLY GROUND BLACK PEPPER
1 TABLESPOON UNSALTED BUTTER
1 TABLESPOON CHOPPED FRESH CILANTRO LEAVES
1/2 CUP GRATED QUESO BLANCO
2 (10-INCH) FLOUR TORTILLAS, WARMED

DIRECTIONS

LOVER A. HEAT THE OIL IN A LARGE SAUTÉ PAN OVER MEDIUM-HIGH HEAT. ADD THE BELL PEPPER, ONION, CORN, JALAPEÑO AND GARLIC. LOWER THE HEAT TO MEDIUM AND COOK THE VEGETABLES UNTIL THEY ARE SOFTENED, ABOUT 10 TO 12 MINUTES. SEASON WITH 1/2 TEASPOON OF THE SALT, REMOVE FROM THE HEAT AND PUT ON A PLATE TO COOL.

LOVER B. WHILE THE VEGETABLES COOL COMBINE THE EGGS, HEAVY CREAM, THE REMAINING 1/2 TEASPOON SALT AND THE BLACK PEPPER. USE A WHISK TO WHIP THE EGGS UNTIL FROTHY.

LOVER A. ADD THE BUTTER TO THE SAUTÉ PAN AND WHEN IT SIZZLES, POUR IN THE BEATEN EGGS. USE A RUBBER SPATULA TO SCRAPE THE SIDES AND BOTTOM OF THE PAN. AFTER 2 MINUTES THE EGGS SHOULD STILL BE SLIGHTLY LOOSE.

LOVER B. SPRINKLE THE CILANTRO OVER THE EGGS, FOLLOWED BY THE GRATED CHEESE, AND REMOVE FROM THE HEAT. FOLD THE EGGS OVER THEMSELVES UNTIL THE CHEESE IS MELTED AND DIVIDE THE EGGS BETWEEN THE TWO TORTILLAS. DIVIDE THE SAUTÉED VEGETABLES BETWEEN THE TORTILLAS, AND FOLD THE LEFT AND RIGHT SIDE OF THE TORTILLA OVER THE CENTER PORTION. ROLL THE BOTTOM EDGE UP TOWARDS THE TOP TO KEEP THE GOODIES IN, AND WRAP A PAPER NAPKIN OR A PIECE OF PARCHMENT AROUND EACH, FOR GOOD MEASURE.

BEST EVER
BLOODY MARY

SERVES 2

INGREDIENTS

3 CUPS TOMATO JUICE

3 TABLESPOONS LEMON JUICE

3 TABLESPOONS LIME JUICE

1 TABLESPOON PREPARED HORSERADISH

1 TABLESPOON WORCESTERSHIRE SAUCE

1 TEASPOON MINCED GARLIC

1 TEASPOON HOT SAUCE

3/4 TEASPOON KOSHER SALT

1/2 TEASPOON FRESHLY GROUND BLACK PEPPER

PREMIUM VODKA

OLIVES, PEPPERONCINI, CUBED CHEESE,

AND OTHER PICKLED VEGETABLES FOR GARNISH

DIRECTIONS

LOVER A. IN A BLENDER COMBINE THE TOMATO JUICE, LEMON JUICE, LIME JUICE, HORSERADISH, WORCESTERSHIRE SAUCE, GARLIC AND HOT SAUCE, AND PROCESS UNTIL SMOOTH.

LOVER B. POUR INTO A NONREACTIVE CONTAINER AND ADD SALT AND BLACK PEPPER TO TASTE. REFRIGERATE UNTIL THOROUGHLY CHILLED.

LOVER A. WHEN READY TO SERVE, FILL EACH GLASS WITH ICE AND 1 TO 2 OUNCES OF VODKA. STIR THE TOMATO JUICE MIXTURE AND POUR IT OVER THE VODKA.

LOVENOTE: SERVE WITH LITTLE RAMEKINS OF PICKLED GARNISHES AND OTHER FINGER NIBBLES.

PANZANELLA SALAD

SERVES 2

THIS CLASSIC RUSTIC BREAD SALAD FROM TUSCANY MAY STIMULATE YOUR IMAGINATION AND
BRING ABOUT VISIONS OF ROLLING HILLS AND ACRES OF GRAPEVINES.

INGREDIENTS

FOR THE VINAIGRETTE:
1 TEASPOON FINELY MINCED GARLIC
1/2 TEASPOON DIJON MUSTARD
3 TABLESPOONS CHAMPAGNE VINEGAR
1/2 CUP EXTRA-VIRGIN OLIVE OIL
1/2 TEASPOON KOSHER SALT
1/4 TEASPOON FRESHLY GROUND BLACK PEPPER

FOR THE BREAD:
3 TABLESPOONS EXTRA-VIRGIN OLIVE OIL
1/2 SMALL FRENCH BREAD (PREFERABLY DAY-OLD), CUT INTO 1-INCH CUBES, OR TORN INTO PIECES
1/2 TEASPOON KOSHER SALT

FOR THE SALAD:
2 LARGE, RIPE TOMATOES, CUT INTO 1-INCH CUBES
1 CUCUMBER, UNPEELED, SEEDED, AND SLICED 1/2-INCH THICK
1/2 RED BELL PEPPER, SEEDED AND DICED
1/2 YELLOW BELL PEPPER, SEEDED AND DICED
1/2 RED ONION, THINLY SLICED
5 LARGE BASIL LEAVES, COARSELY CHOPPED
1/4 CUP PITTED OLIVES
1 TABLESPOON CAPERS, DRAINED

DIRECTIONS

LOVER A. PREPARE THE VINAIGRETTE, WHISKING ALL THE INGREDIENTS TOGETHER IN A SMALL BOWL.

LOVER B. HEAT THE 3 TABLESPOONS OIL IN A LARGE SAUTÉ PAN. ADD THE BREAD AND SALT AND COOK OVER MEDIUM-LOW HEAT, TOSSING FREQUENTLY, FOR 6 TO 8 MINUTES, OR UNTIL NICELY BROWNED. YOU MAY HAVE TO DO THIS IN BATCHES SO THAT THE BREAD DOESN'T BURN. REMOVE FROM THE PAN WITH A SLOTTED SPOON.

LOVER A. IN A LARGE BOWL COMBINE THE TOMATOES, CUCUMBER, RED PEPPER, YELLOW PEPPER, RED ONION, BASIL, OLIVES AND CAPERS. ADD THE BREAD CUBES OR TORN PIECES TO THE SALAD AND TOSS WITH THE VINAIGRETTE. SEASON TO TASTE WITH SALT AND PEPPER. ALLOW THE SALAD TO SIT FOR ABOUT 30 MINUTES FOR THE FLAVORS TO BLEND.

LOVENOTE: IF YOU LIKE WILTED SALADS, THIS WOULD BE EVEN BETTER THE NEXT DAY.

VANILLASKY

SERVES 2

INGREDIENTS

6 OUNCES VANILLA FLAVORED VODKA

2 OUNCE STRAWBERRY LIQUEUR

2 OUNCE CRANBERRY-PINEAPPLE JUICE

SPLASH OF CHAMPAGNE

DIRECTIONS

LOVER A. COMBINE THE VODKA, LIQUEUR AND CRANPINEAPPLE JUICE.

LOVER B. DIVIDE BETWEEN TWO GLASSES AND TOP WITH CHAMPAGNE.

LOVENOTE: MMMM.

WHITE CHOCOLATE DIPPED STRAWBERRIES

SERVES 2

STRAWBERRIES AND CHOCOLATE SPELL LO-O-OVE.

INGREDIENTS

1 12 OUNCE BAG WHITE CHOCOLATE CHIPS

1 TABLESPOON SHORTENING

8 LARGE RIPE STRAWBERRIES, WITH STEMS IF POSSIBLE

1/2 CUP SEMISWEET CHOCOLATE CHIPS

1 TEASPOON SHORTENING

DIRECTIONS

LOVER A. LINE A COOKIE SHEET WITH WAXED PAPER. HEAT THE WHITE CHOCOLATE AND 1 TABLESPOON SHORTENING IN A MEDIUM SAUCEPAN OVER LOW HEAT, STIRRING CONSTANTLY UNTIL CHIPS ARE MELTED.

LOVER B. FOR EACH STRAWBERRY, POKE A FORK OR TOOTHPICK INTO THE STEM END, AND DIP THREE-FOURTHS OF THE WAY INTO THE MELTED WHITE CHOCOLATE, LEAVING THE TOP OF THE STRAWBERRY AND LEAVES UNCOATED. PLACE ON WAXED PAPER-COVERED COOKIE SHEET, POINT DOWN, STEM UP.

LOVER A. HEAT THE SEMISWEET CHOCOLATE CHIPS AND 1 TEASPOON SHORTENING IN A SMALL SAUCEPAN OVER LOW HEAT, STIRRING CONSTANTLY UNTIL THE CHOCOLATE IS MELTED.

LOVERS A AND B. DRIZZLE MELTED SEMISWEET CHOCOLATE IN A ZIGZAG OVER DIPPED STRAWBERRIES, USING A SMALL SPOON. REFRIGERATE UNCOVERED ABOUT 30 MINUTES OR UNTIL COATING IS SET.

LOVENOTE: TAKE TURNS POPPING THESE INTO EACH OTHER'S MOUTH FOR SOME SCHMOOZY, GIGGLING FUN.

SWEET ONION,
HAM & CHEESE
FRITTATA

SERVES 2

INGREDIENTS

2 TABLESPOONS UNSALTED BUTTER

1/2 LARGE SWEET ONION, SLICED

1/2 TEASPOON KOSHER SALT

FRESHLY GROUND BLACK PEPPER

4 LARGE EGGS

1/4 CUP MILK

1/2 CUP DICED HAM

1 TABLESPOON MINCED CHIVES

1 CUP GRATED SWISS CHEESE

DIRECTIONS

LOVER A. POSITION A RACK ABOUT 6-10 INCHES FROM THE BROILER AND TURN ON THE HEAT. IT'S YOUR TURN TO PREPARE THE MIMOSAS, SO START SQUEEZING A PAIR OF ORANGES.

LOVER B. MELT THE BUTTER IN A MEDIUM NON-STICK SKILLET OVER MEDIUM HEAT. ADD THE ONIONS AND SEASON WITH A PINCH OF SALT AND PEPPER. LOWER THE HEAT AND COOK SLOWLY, STIRRING OCCASIONALLY, UNTIL THE ONIONS ARE SOFT AND GOLDEN, ABOUT 15 MINUTES. TRANSFER THE ONIONS TO A BOWL TO COOL.

LOVER A. WHISK THE EGGS AND MILK IN A MEDIUM BOWL WITH THE REMAINING SALT AND PEPPER UNTIL SMOOTH. STIR THE ONIONS, HAM, CHIVES AND CHEESE INTO THE EGGS.

LOVER B. INCREASE THE HEAT TO MEDIUM UNDER THE BUTTER IN THE SKILLET. WHEN THE BUTTER IS SIZZLING, POUR THE FRITTATA MIXTURE INTO THE PAN AND STIR GENTLY TO MAKE SURE THE FILLINGS ARE EVENLY DISTRIBUTED. COOK UNTIL THE BOTTOM IS SET, ABOUT 5 MINUTES. SLIDE THE SKILLET UNDER THE BROILER AND COOK UNTIL THE EGGS ARE SET AND GOLDEN BROWN, ABOUT 5-6 MINUTES. REMOVE FROM THE OVEN, COVER AND SET ASIDE FOR 5 MINUTES.

LOVER A. UNCORK A BOTTLE OF CHILLED CHAMPAGNE. POUR THE FRESHLY-SQUEEZED ORANGE JUICE INTO TWO STEM GLASSES. TOP EACH WITH CHAMPAGNE AND A MARASCHINO CHERRY.

LOVER B. INVERT THE FRITTATA ONTO A LARGE PLATE OR PLATTER. CUT INTO WEDGES.

SEXYOLD FASHIONED

SERVES 2

THERE'S SOMETHING TO BE SAID FOR BEING SEXY AND
OLD FASHIONED, DON'T YOU THINK?

INGREDIENTS

3 OUNCES WHISKEY, YOUR FAVORITE KIND

2 OUNCES BOURBON

1/2 OUNCE BÉNÉDICTINE LIQUEUR

6 DASHES ANGOSTURA BITTERS

2 TEASPOONS SIMPLE SYRUP

ORANGE PEEL FOR GARNISH

DIRECTIONS

LOVER A. COMBINE INGREDIENTS IN A MIXING GLASS AND STIR BRIEFLY WITH ICE CUBES UNTIL CHILLED.

LOVER B. PLACE A LARGE ICE CUBE INTO TWO OLD FASHIONED GLASSES AND POUR THE DRINK OVER. GARNISH WITH THE STRIP OF ORANGE PEEL.

LET'S DO IT AGAIN...

ISBN 978-0-9909-716-3-4

FIRST PRINTING 2015
COPYRIGHT MAXIMUM FLAVOR, INC © 2015
ALAIN MARTINEZ, LLC ©2015

AUTHOR / CHEF: ADRIANNE CALVO
AUTHOR/ PHOTOGRAPHER: ALAIN MARTINEZ
EXECUTIVE PRODUCER: ALAIN MARTINEZ
COPYWRITER: JESSIE TIRSCH
DESIGN BY MELANNIE MORFA

SPECIAL THANKS TO:
EYVIS MENDOZA
PETER MARRERO
JORDAN MARTINEZ
GISELLE GUTIERREZ
VANESSA GONZALEZ
MARZ MAKEUP & HAIR

FACEBOOK.COM/CHEFADRIANNE
TWITTER.COM/CHEFADRIANNE
INSTAGRAM.COM/CHEFADRIANNE
CHEFADRIANNES.COM
ADRIANNECALVO.COM
MAKEITCOUNTCHARITIES.ORG

FACEBOOK.COM/ALAINMARTINEZPHOTOGRAPHY
TWITTER.COM/ALAINMARTINEZ
INSTAGRAM.COM/ALAINMARTINEZPHOTO
ALAINMARTINEZ.COM

CPSIA information can be obtained at www.ICGtesting.com
Printed in the USA
LVIW01n0711290115
424790LV00001B/1